Walking Back to Happiness

Finding ourselves in France

Penelope Swithinbank

Sarah
GRACE
PUBLISHING
Dyslexic Friendly

Endorsements

More than a tale of a bucket-list adventure, this is a return-to-love story of a marriage grown cold. Walking miles across France, our protagonists inch closer towards each other. With colour and grit, Walking Back to Happiness shows what can be regained in a relationship when we commit to walking a new path side-by-side.

Sheridan Voysey, writer/speaker/broadcaster, author of *The Making of Us: Who We Can Become When Life Doesn't Go as Planned* and *Resurrection Year: Turning Broken Dreams into New Beginnings*

Crossing France from coast to coast on foot, Penelope becomes reacquainted with the husband she fell in love with and makes peace with the pain and trauma of the previous years. This is a travelogue in the best tradition, full of evocative descriptions of landscape, architecture and locals, as well as vivid accounts of epic gastronomic experiences that will make your mouth water. The reflections on marriage, forgiveness and the spirituality of suffering are deeply moving, as is the sheer determination and courage it takes for the couple to pull on their boots and keep going each morning. You will be uplifted, cheered and inspired by this book. And maybe even tempted to go for a longer-than-usual walk...

Jo Swinney, author of *Home: the quest to belong*

I unknowingly finished *Walking Back to Happiness* on Penelope and Kim's forty-second wedding anniversary. That's fitting, for as she so movingly recounts, their great walk across France helped them journey back to a loving and fruitful partnership. Poignant and constructive, it's one to enjoy and ponder – perhaps from the comfort of your home!
Amy Boucher Pye, author of *Finding Myself in Britain*

Walking Back to Happiness puts one in mind of The Unlikely Pilgrimage of Harold Frye. With the use of vivid details, humour, and vulnerability, Penelope takes us on a heart-warming journey that will not only provoke you to book a walking holiday, but think more deeply about love and commitment.
Shelly Miller, author of *Rhythms of Rest: Finding the Spirit of Sabbath in a Busy World*

Hippocrates, the father of modern medicine, famously said that 'walking is man's best medicine.' I doubt you'll ever see this more graphically confirmed than in *Walking Back to Happiness* - a tale of four sore feet, two frail hearts, and one life-changing walk. As you read, you'll find yourself journeying with Penelope and Kim across France. By the time you sit with them on the seashore at the end, the sea fret of the Atlantic Ocean on your face, maybe you too will taste the medicine they received.
Mark Stibbe, bestselling and award-winning author of *Home at Last* and *King of Hearts*

Wow, what a book! A real feast for the senses, where the scenery, food and feelings all jump off the page and transport you to France. This book is charming and captivating, enchanting and exhilarating - I feel as if I've walked this beautiful route myself (with the benefit of no blisters) just by reading this delicious, descriptive and transformative book. Penelope's writing is stunning, it stirs your soul, awakens your desire for travel and adventure and will also make you laugh on more than one occasion (the image of Penelope squatting to relieve herself whilst also wearing pearls, and then at a separate time reapplying her lipstick, spoke to me as deeply as the more reflective, spiritual anecdotes). It's simply a wonderful read that I already want to revisit! I cannot recommend this book enough - it's simply stunning.

Sally Beaton, author of *Women with Sparkle*

For Robin, Harriet and Victoria
Your love, support and encouragement
mean the world to me

Acknowledgements

Just as it takes a village to raise a child, so it takes a community or group to write a book and I could not have done this without the help and encouragement of so many family members and friends. I'm grateful and blessed to have wonderful people in my life who have taken an interest, cheered me on, asked for the story of our Walk.

Miles Moreland wrote a book about his epic journey in the 1980s, which gave me the original inspiration, and he then kindly spurred me on with emails along the way. Trevor from ATP Health and Fitness keeps me fit twice a week and explained how to train for the long distance backpacking. Cherith Stibbe, Susan Alexander Yates, Amy Boucher Pye, Margaret Doyle, Tim Dewes, and Sarah Grace, my wonderful and very patient publisher, gave me valuable feedback on the initial raw manuscript and encouraged me to keep going. Mark Stibbe at BookLab read it – and told me my writing reminded him of the Evelyn Waugh book I was reading while in France; I took it as a compliment, but he edited out all my erudition and made it readable for you. I'm actually now very grateful!

My thanks to those who read the manuscript and wrote kind endorsements, and to all the social media friends who read our daily online posts and weekly blogs and cheered us on and told us to keep going – and then asked for the book of the adventures. Thank you.

Most of all, thanks to those who have supported us through the hard times of the past few years. You know who you are and both of us are immensely grateful. We would not have made it without your prayers, love and support.

However, the most important and deepest gratitude is for my children and their spouses – Robin and Rachel, Harriet and Stephen, Victoria and Gene. Please know how much you mean to me: I could not have done any of this without you and, of course, your children, my fabulous grandchildren – Talitha, Jonah, William, Bethia, Sophie and Toby. They are so wonderful and I should have had them first.

Kim. Thank you for walking with me. Thank you for putting up with me. I am so proud of you and all you are doing to rebuild and restore. We have had over forty-two years of marriage now, and I pray there are many more still to come. I am so glad that we found ourselves in France and can continue to walk together in the same direction. Let's have another Great Adventure soon!

Contents

Preamble
A Great Walk

'Portugal? Portugal? You want to go to Portugal by taxi?'

The taxi driver outside the airport at Béziers in south-west France is incredulous. He summons his fellow drivers around him to repeat our destination and they howl with laughter at our mispronunciation of Portiragnes. My husband, Kim, repeats it authoritatively in French:

'*Non, non, Portiragnes. Portiragnes-plage, s'il vous plaît,*' he says again. 'We want to go to Portiragnes Beach, please.'

It is the start of our Big Adventure: to walk from the Mediterranean to the Atlantic across France, from the Languedoc through Midi-Pyrenees and then Aquitaine. It is a mere 530 km, more or less. 330 miles. 20,908,800 inches. We will feel every single one. But it will change us in ways we could never have imagined.

The Great Walk – *la Grande Randonnée* – has been on my bucket list for nearly thirty years after reading Miles Moreland's book recounting his own grand marathon across the south-west of France. And I love walking, especially with a dog.

It began with dog walks when I was a ten-year-old, getting up early on summer mornings to sneak out of the house with our family Springer Spaniel and walk her with a friend in the woods near our homes. And as a teenager, when we had moved to live near the sea, there was nothing better than tramping across the fields to the beach, black Labrador in tow, and usually by myself. The freedom and the fresh air were life-giving to a rather solitary teenager. Later, with a clergy husband and a home and family of my own, I walked the streets of Norwich pushing my 'stately pram of England', a baby asleep in the pram, a toddler on the seat on top and an older toddler on the shopping tray underneath, my own dog, a golden Cocker Spaniel, trotting along beside me. We walked to the shops and the shopping was stowed all around the children; we walked to the park and the children played on the swings; we walked to nursery school.

Then, after another move close to my parents-in-law, we walked to prep school near Bath. We moved to Stamford, for twelve happy years in The Rectory, and the children walked by themselves to school and I took the yellow Labrador Ollie on long rambles across the fields or by the river.

And when the children grew up and left home, my husband and I began walking together on weeklong holidays in Italy – Casteluccia to Spoleto, Todi to Assisi, the Amalfi Coast; together we led pilgrimages on the Via Francigena, from San Gimignano to Siena or on to Montalcino. I organised pilgrimages on the Cotswold Way for groups of women, doing the 100 miles from Chipping Campden to Bath in six days and discovering the difference it makes physically, spiritually, emotionally, to walk for days on end, leaving the stress of normal everyday life for a while, concentrating on the countryside and the peace and the sheer rhythm of placing one foot in front of another.

And how the silence and the solitude leave more space for the still small voice of God.

One day, my husband Kim and I promised ourselves, one day we will walk together across France from the Mediterranean to the Atlantic.

And here we are. Sitting in a taxi on our way from the airport to the Mediterranean, excited, scared – and, if we are honest, a little lost in our marriage and our lives.

'For whatever we lose (like a you or a me) it's always ourself we find in the sea.' (e.e. cummings)

Will we really walk from sea to sea? And will we find ourselves and each other again in France?

Chapter One
Finding the Route

Preparing to do a Great Walk focuses the mind wonderfully. And makes me realise that gentle Sunday-afternoon strolls are one thing, but walking three hundred and thirty miles carrying a heavy backpack is something totally different.

A long hike once a week needs to become the norm – eight to ten miles might be a good rehearsal.

But things do not go according to plan.

Originally we had planned to retire in July and do The Great Walk Across France two months later; but the selling of the listed property we were using as a Christian retreat house took a further whole year, with new planning permissions imposed by the local conservation officer causing headaches and money and building work. The stress must have contributed to Kim having a stroke very unexpectedly, followed by ocular shingles. Fortunately the stroke left no physical impairment, but he suffered dyslexia-like symptoms and great tiredness. The Walk was put on hold.

Ruby Wedding Celebrations

We eventually moved house a whole year later; two weeks after that, it was our Ruby Wedding anniversary and we planned to start The Walk in late August at the Atlantic and walk to the Mediterranean, as a celebration of our anniversary and new retirement. But Kim played tennis with our son at our anniversary celebrations and tore his Achilles tendon badly. The Great Walk was put on hold yet again.

Recovering from a torn Achilles takes a long time and a lot of patience and weeks and weeks in a specialist boot, which had to be worn twenty-four hours a day. Kim showed amazing fortitude to begin with but became bored and frustrated when ill health was compounded by a diagnosis of both flu and pneumonia over the Christmas holidays. I am no nurse; my patience is limited, my frustrations and lack of understanding are shameful. He had little to do; I had no consideration for what he had had to endure for some time.

All this on top of the previous dreadful year. And several tough years prior to that. There were failures and bad decisions. The strains of life and ministry had led Kim to a dark and very unhappy place, putting enormous pressure on our marriage. Some years previously, he had had what used to be termed a mental breakdown; now, there was physical illness to deal with as well.

We drifted apart in every way, including a time of actual separation. After the affectionate and joyous renewing of our wedding vows on the day of our fortieth wedding anniversary in the presence of our family and the bishop, we had turned our backs on one another instead of supporting and helping one another. I sent him away; told him it was a six-week period for him to sort himself out and for me to learn to forgive a whole lot of pain caused over the past several years of his dark places.

He left. He stayed with friends at first, then went to Portugal to find some sun and to play golf; he prayed, thought, reflected.

I went on retreat for a few days to Ty Mawr, an Anglican convent on the edge of Wales. It was a mild February; snowdrops covered the ground; I read and reflected each morning, walked in the afternoons along the Wye Valley, attended evening chapel services and talked with an understanding, Spirit-filled nun. I felt that during this Lenten period I was to *fast from recrimination and feast on forgiveness*. I'm not sure where that phrase originated – there was certainly a Scripture reading in the chapel that included some words about recriminations; and it was Lent so there was fasting. The phrase slipped into my mind and it stuck and became of utmost importance to me over the weeks and months ahead. God-given, perhaps.

Then, another day and another service in the chapel, and the reading was from Mark.

> *'Then, calling the crowd to join his disciples, Jesus said, "If any of you wants to be my follower, you must give up your own way, take up your cross, and follow me."'* (Mark 8:34 NLT)

And again, something slipped into my mind: I was to take up my cross gratefully, even joyfully, and not sullenly and resentfully as I had been doing. Instead of thinking, 'Why me? Why us? Why do I have to carry this particular cross which strikes at the heart of all I hold dear?' I began to realise that it was what was asked of me, that I needed to learn to ask, 'Why NOT me? What might I need to learn in and through all of this?' And I caught a glimpse of what others may also be carrying – not the same cross, but nevertheless a cross which humbles or hurts them, makes them stagger, holds them back, and is probably never aired in public.

'You and me both,' I realised, seeing people in a new way. I felt humbled, grateful, renewed.

There are two copies of Henri Nouwen's *The Return of the Prodigal* on our bookshelves; we took one each and separately devoured every word, thought, teaching. It became our book of the year, of the moment. And when later in May we led a pilgrimage together on the Celtic Cornish path for a group of Americans, it became the basis for our talks and meditations. Each of us has to be the repentant younger son, making that Great Walk home; each of us has elements of 'elder brotherishness' within us, petulant, jealous, judging; each of us is called to be like the father, welcoming home the prodigal, watching and waiting and forgiving.

As I read, I tried to imagine how Kim must be feeling and thinking as he too read this book. Did he see himself as the younger son who ran away? Did he yearn for the welcome home the father offers? And it dawned on me that God was calling *me* to offer that welcome. It was for *me* to forgive and to extend a welcome on behalf of Father God. Suddenly I wanted to be the hands of the father as Rembrandt portrayed them – placed lovingly on the back of the shoulders of the prodigal, pulling him closer, the hands saying what perhaps the voice struggles to convey. Nouwen writes movingly about the hands in Rembrandt's painting. He thinks Rembrandt purposely portrayed two different hands, one male and one female, expressing the different aspects of a loving God. That appealed to me. Could I go back and welcome Kim home as God welcomes all prodigals, including me?

After nearly four weeks, I invited Kim to come home. He was surprised, pleased, overwhelmed. Unsure of what it would look like. As we sat face-to-face via the computers, I could see the look of astonishment pass across his face, followed by delight and perhaps a little uncertainty: this was two weeks early.

'Are you sure?' he asked me. I was close to tears. I missed him. I wanted him home more than I wanted to hang on to the pain of yet more failure. The salutary separation, brief as it was, had actually drawn us closer, because it made us want to work on the problems and the difficulties. Supported lovingly and prayerfully by our family and a few close friends, we began the long journey back to closeness. We felt that a loving heavenly Father was graciously doing some work in each of us.

So Kim booked an earlier flight home from Portugal, and late one evening he came in the front door at home. I ran down the stairs to greet him, and he walked across the hall to where I waited on the bottom step. It made it easier for me to reach to his tall shoulders and place my hands on to his upper back, just as I had planned and hoped to do, drawing him closer to me.

He was home.

Inwardly, I forgave him and welcomed him in. Outwardly, we stood in silence as I embraced him, my hands on his back in the way Rembrandt portrayed. It was a special, private moment.

Might the Great Walk be a good way to continue this journey? Might we find ourselves again in France?

'Let's do it soon!' we said to each other. 'June? That gives us three months to get ready. Let's GO!'

So we did.

Preparations Really Begin

Kim carried his golf clubs around the course each week. I loaded up my backpack with heavy towels and books and tramped the countryside. We began looking at possible routes – far enough south to be a narrower part of France but not so far south that we were in the foothills of the Pyrenees. We decided to start at the Mediterranean in early June and walk west, hopefully avoiding having to walk in too much heat. Kim used his technological skills and the internet to download all kinds of useful information. French walking maps of *Les Grandes Randonnées*, the footpaths that traverse France. Bed and breakfast sites. The French equivalent of Ordinance Survey Maps. Other useful information.

He began to plan a possible route. There had to be no more than 15–19 miles a day, somewhere to stay each evening – a problem when a long way from towns and larger villages – plus a nice place for a rest day every week. And as few roads as possible. He also downloaded the Michel Thomas advanced French conversation course and began a daily session, determined to be able to converse a little if we met anyone on our adventure. The maps and the course were each to prove to be lifesaving at different times.

I researched which foods provide most energy – and vowed to eat a lot of fresh salmon, eggs, tinned tuna, almonds, yoghurt, spinach, pumpkin seeds. In fact, we saw little or nothing of any of them!

We checked our walking gear again. A visit to our daughter in America meant an outing to REI, the specialists in outdoor equipment. We bought extra-lightweight shoes for evening wear, waterproof clothing and backpack covers, easy-dry underwear and shirts and shorts, internal waterproof bags for packing things separately. And a camping washing line with integral 'pegs'. Small sprays of anti-mozzie, ant-fly and suntan lotion; of antiseptic and blister plasters and ibruprofen. It wasn't that France didn't stock such things; we wanted lightweight small containers that were easy to pack and carry, and we didn't want to spend hours hunting them down during the Walk. Here they all were, under one roof.

Flights were booked to Bézier for June 1st and then back from Bordeaux, including three days extra at the end 'just in case'. Training began in earnest with test runs of loading the backpacks and walking with them.

They were heavy.

I had to reassess. I laid every single item on our big double bed, spread it out and then considered.

Was it needed?

Was it important?

Could I do without it for a few weeks?

What was truly life-giving?

And which were the lightest items?

I was literally weighing things in each hand, trying to decide what I really had to carry and what was just a luxury. Not one for camping (there's nowhere to hang my frocks and the bathroom facilities are not to my high standards) I am not used to travelling light. Makeup? Only the basics: moisturiser and mascara. More than two not-walking evening outfits? Unnecessary. Definitely no books, just a Kindle. Only one sweater (I was to regret that decision). I even had to weigh journals to find the lightest one possible that would still have sufficient pages for four weeks of new experiences.

Eventually, we whittled everything down to 22.7lbs for Kim, and 17.2lbs for me – plus my small waist pack. And those pounds didn't include the water we would need to carry each day.

Raising Money for Charity

One of the things we wanted to do was to ask friends and acquaintances to sponsor the Great Walk. We have two favourite charities: The International Justice Mission, which works to bring justice particularly in areas of human trafficking and which was founded by Gary Haugen, a member of our congregation at the church where we served while living in the USA; and People Against Poverty, with which our local church has strong links and has mission trips to Romania. The social media postings began, with the hashtags #MedtoAtlantic #WalkacrossFrance #gapyearfinalfling #findingourselvesinFrance.

Friends and family were amazed when we told them what we planned to do. Some asked us what we would do if we got halfway and found ourselves lost or stuck or unable to walk another step. Others were aghast and perhaps considered us to be insane. But gradually our answers seemed to reassure them, and soon everyone was cheering us on, or at least feigning enthusiasm and excitement in order to appear supportive of our crazy idea. But lots of people were incredibly generous in giving to our chosen charities, sending us encouraging messages or their favourite remedy for blisters.

And sometimes seeming just a little envious of our grand idea and our freedom to be able to do this.

Honestly, there *were* times when anxiety nibbled at our heels, when ambivalence kept us awake at night, when fear of attempting to walk too far in our mid-sixties gave us reason to hesitate.

Could we *really* do this?

Final Countdown

But the flights are booked, the accommodation is finalised and, suddenly, it's Wednesday May 30th! The last day but one before departure. We are almost overwhelmed with excitement and yet daunted at the same time. The original vision, all the planning, the summoning up of courage and determination, is about to pay off.

Until Wednesday afternoon.

Kim has a colonoscopy scheduled for Wednesday afternoon, thinking it would be routine; but some polyps have to be removed and his body reacts very badly. He sleeps the rest of the evening.

On Thursday, the last day at home, he feels really poorly and lacking in energy and distinctly under the weather. It doesn't bode well for Friday's flight. And the post doesn't bring the extra walking socks he had ordered, so as we do a final repack late on Thursday afternoon Kim remembers the lack of socks, leading to a mad dash into Bath at closing time to find alternatives. He has large feet – VERY large feet – socks in his size are hard to find.

At last, finally, everything is ready. We're too excited to sleep. And it's hot in our bedroom under the eaves. One of the hottest summers ever, in England. Will it be hot in France too? And have we really packed everything? What have we forgotten? Are we really and truly going to do this?

Walking in the Air

Friday June 1st arrives cool, grey and misty. Read fog: flight delays forecast for Bristol airport, the second highest airport in the UK. I feel surprisingly calm. I do a last load of washing, empty the bins, rush around for a last-minute check. We will be away for five weeks and Sarah and Nathan, a young missionary couple home on furlough, will be house-sitting for us during our time away.

Classic FM is playing quietly in the background and asks for requests. I text about our walk and the money we are hoping to raise for charity and ask them to play Mendelssohn's 'War March of the Priests'. It was the music we chose for leaving the church at the end of our wedding nearly forty-one years ago and it seems even more appropriate today. Aled Jones plays it for us and wishes us good luck.

'We should be walking in the air now,' Kim says. He has a great sense of humour.

We dress in full walking gear for the flight, including boots just in case our luggage should be delayed or lost. Everything else is easily replaceable but not the right personal walking gear. It feels slightly odd to be dressed for walking, but it impresses our taxi driver. He cheerfully shoulders our heavy packs as if they weigh nothing, and tosses them into the boot of his car – but he's probably twenty years younger than we are.

We take selfies as we stand on the doorstep and lock the door behind us. It will be over a month until we return. Gulp.

And We're Off!

'How are you feeling?' Kim whispers to me in the back seat under cover of the car radio.

'Slightly scared, slightly daunted, slightly nauseous with lack of sleep coupled with nerves!' I reply, trying to laugh. He squeezes my hand as I swallow hard and look out of the window at the passing landscape. Even this early in the summer, it's looking parched after the dry, warm spring. 'What will it look like in five weeks' time – always supposing we last that long?' I wonder aloud.

Kim laughs. 'The return flights are booked and I'm not paying to change them.' He's always the optimist. I like to think I'm the realist but it's probably more like the pessimist. Yet I am determined to do this Walk.

At least, I hope I am.

We shrink-wrap our backpacks at check-in, with the large roll Kim had ordered online.

'Are you worried about security?' asks an anxious fellow backpacker, watching us. We assure him we are merely concerned about our straps and buckles, not wanting them torn off in the hold by baggage handling. I'm stopped at security. I've forgotten there's a 'useful implement' in my waist bag. It's a small but useful 10-in-1 tool. Bother. I'd packed everything as it would be for walking and not for security! It's taken from me, with the assurance it can be collected at a vast price on my return to the airport.

Meanwhile, our flight is delayed an hour. We fight through the seething hordes of hopeful holiday-makers and buy expensive bottled water after failing to find a water fountain to fill our own bottles. Bristol airport appears not to be environmentally friendly. I decide I need a fabulous lipstick to keep me somewhat human and civilised during the walk, and dash into duty free and buy nearly the first one I see at my favourite beauty counter.

An immediate application boosts morale enormously.

Landing at Béziers airport after flying in low over the rugby ground and the bullring, we anxiously await our packs. But they arrive safely and we then have to spend some time trying to remove the shrink-wrap so that we can shoulder them again. We need the confiscated tool; only it would have been inside the shrink-wrapped pack. But eventually it's all removed, and we step outside into the warm French sun and take a taxi to Portiragnes-Plage to check into the tiny hotel.

The balcony has a sideways view of the Mediterranean, and we crane our necks to catch a glimpse of our starting point.

'This is it,' I say in amazement. 'We're really here and we are really going to do this Walk!' I can scarcely believe it.

An Evening by the Sea

We change out of our walking clothes and boots, and run down to the ocean to dip our feet in the cool ripples of surf. Our feet are touching the Mediterranean waters and it will save having to take off our walking boots when we are here again tomorrow morning; and we don't want to walk with sand between our toes. The late afternoon sun is still faintly warm; there are wispy clouds floating about, a slight haze hovering over the long, flat shingle-and-sand beach. A few families are determinedly still playing and there are a couple of brave souls in the water. There is minimal surf and splash and even I, with my dislike of water and hate of swimming, am happy to remove my flip-flops and stand at the edge of the ocean.

'Tomorrow we walk!' we say to each other. We still can't really believe that we are actually going to start walking from here and keep going until we reach the Atlantic.

There's a little wooden shack calling itself a beach bar, painted with peeling cream-and-blue stripes.

'Let's have a celebratory glass of something,' Kim suggests, and we sit on the rickety plastic chairs and treat ourselves to a glass of Muscat each. It comes in plastic cups and we linger to watch the evening fall. Our talk inevitably turns to our hopes and fears for the next few weeks. About the state of our marriage and the state of Kim's leg after the torn Achilles tendon eleven months ago. About who we are, individually and together.

'It used to be us against the rest of the world,' I whisper to him. 'And it will be again,' he promises.

The past two years have been hard, stressful, inharmonious years for many reasons. Running a retreat house in north Wiltshire, in a sixteenth-century farmhouse we had renovated lovingly and prayerfully, had proved to be both exhausting in every way and unsustainable financially. It also put a huge strain on our marriage, and on Kim's health, as we struggled to maintain the house, provide for guests, market and advertise to find new ones, and make the finances work. Perhaps naively, we felt that we had been called by God to do this ministry and that the Lord would therefore provide everything needed, including the money and the strength and everything else.

Looking back now, maybe it was simply our way of trying to escape an extremely unhappy time in north London when Kim was rector of a large evangelical church. Neither of us thrived. Kim was going through mental anguish following the death of his mother, which had in turn brought up a lot of past pain and wounding from being 'abandoned' by her at boarding school from the age of seven. His 'boarded heart' was broken and had never had the opportunity for healing in that area. We all cope with pain in different ways. For the stiff-upper-lipped Englishman, difficulties and pain are often suppressed, pushed down and ignored until something causes the anguish to rear up and overflow. Kim's swept him into a deep, dark place which he tried, probably unsuccessfully, to hide again. It's only looking back now that I can see the devastating mental breakdown. He pushed that down too, or so he thought. I knew that he had changed, that I couldn't get through to him, that we were drifting apart.

Eventually, we left the London parish – and perhaps should have done so earlier, as soon as we realised that it was not the place for us. Within ten months of arriving in London we knew it wasn't working, that it was causing mental anguish for Kim and deep unhappiness for us both. It takes courage to accept, as clergy, that you are not a 'good fit' and to walk away before it all gets too much.

Or maybe it's pride that keeps you there, unwilling to admit you can't cope because you are unhappy and it just isn't working in the way you had prayed and planned and hoped. We talked of leaving within a few months of arriving; felt that to do so after less than a year would be perceived as failure, as letting people down, as not being obedient to a call of God. Had it been his calling? Would it have been better to have stayed in America and looked for something there?

Yet now, in retrospect, I begin to realise that where one lives, what one does, are perhaps secondary issues. The main thing is my relationship with the Lord, deepening and developing it, and leaving anywhere or anything which detracts from it, even if the world doesn't understand, or criticises that leaving. The time in London took each of us away from the Lord, contributed to deep anguish and loneliness and, for some reason, caused us to turn our backs on each other, with devastating results. Now, at last, we can talk about these things, acknowledge them, ask for forgiveness from each other and from God. We hold hands and feel closer to each other than we have for some time.

Wandering back to the Promenade, we have the first of many evening meals out – five whole weeks of not cooking, I think gleefully. And then realise that all the eating out could add pounds to my weight. I opt for a goats' cheese salad.

This Is It

Kim wakes me at 7.30am from a deep pill-induced sleep. My heart had been racing at 11pm and I was breathless with anticipation, fear, anxiety, excitement. We pack, excited to get going. What takes me fifteen minutes this first morning will be down to five in a few days, but this is the first time I have to fit everything back into the green waterproof inner bags and then wedge the bags into the pack.

A tiny, very-limited-choice buffet breakfast in the hotel is €10 each. A steep learning curve. Monsieur is given our phones to take our photo on the hotel step as we leave, and we cross the car park and head for the steps leading down to the sand, looking for someone to take our photo on the beach. There's a meditating black-lycra-clad cyclist sitting cross-legged on the bench, his bike propped beside him, his face turned to the sun. We wait for him to open his eyes and as we stand with our backs to the Mediterranean and our faces towards the Atlantic, he obligingly manipulates the smartphone camera.

And so it begins – 530 km to our destination. Will we really do it?

Kim takes both my hands in his.

'Time for our own meditation,' he says. 'I'd like to begin each day's walk with a prayer.'

And so we commit this day, this walk, this marriage, each other, to God.

And then we're off! We're going to cross the Languedoc, the region in the deepest south-west France, nestled against the Pyrenees. *Lonely Planet* named the region as one of its top 5 places to visit in 2018, and we've each read and loved Kate Mosse's series of books set in the region in the time of the Cathars. It's a great choice for us for many reasons, not least because we love it so and visited for a few weeks the year before, house-sitting for some friends who live near Mirepoix.

Along the pavement, around the little town, in the cool of the morning, striding with purpose and excitement. We're headed to the Canal du Midi and at 8.45am it's a pleasant temperature for walking. As we reach the canal, several boats chug past us. We play hare and tortoise with a yellow-and-white *bateau* all morning. We feel confident and content.

'This is easy! Hope it's like this the whole way,' I say confidently, striding along easily.

The path by the canal is well trodden, sometimes gravel, sometimes tarmac, occasionally grassy. Sometimes there are low banks between us and the canal, full of wild flowers and grasses; occasionally there's just a narrow strip of ground. With the canal on our right, and little houses and gardens on our left, we look across the water to plane trees and willows lining the opposite bank. The canal is full, due to recent rains, and the boats ride high.

'The water has its own particular smell,' I say, sniffing at the cool, damp air.

'Yes, wet, musty, and not over pleasant,' Kim agrees. But I can scent water and freshness and grass, while gazing at plane trees and rambling roses. It feels very French.

Suddenly a bicycle overtakes us, barely missing me. It's the first of many. They buzz us all morning, almost touching me, with no warning bell or shout when approaching from behind. They come so quickly that I don't hear them and there's no time to leap out of the way. And as Kim is ahead most of the morning, it's my back they are targeting. But I don't need to use my walking stick on the towpath as it's flat and easy walking; instead it becomes a protective weapon, held pointing out from me and ensuring that cyclists have to steer clear. It seems to be the only way to prevent them crashing into us. Bikes rule – OK?

KIM:
There are definitely generational differences on the boats. Interestingly, a yellow boat is driven by an older Aussie (we think that's the accent) and a 60-plus-year-old wife. She does all the work tying the boat up and he sits there in splendid isolation doing the technical stuff of driving the boat. The boat behind has a strapping young man and a gorgeous young blonde in a bikini in her 20s or 30s. And she drives and he does all the work. I think things have changed.

A vast sheet of scarlet greets us as we round a bend of the canal: across the water, through the plane trees, a rising field of poppies leads up to a tin silhouette of a bull.

Pleasure boats pass up and down. It feels good to be walking, but our feet are already suffering on the tarmac. And Kim is yearning for a real ice cream, preferably artisanal, handmade, delicious.

Rebuilding Begins

As we walk, we talk. And we confess and acknowledge how tired and fed up we've been with each other recently; how short tempered; and how the worry of the removal of the polyps last week had caused each of us to clam up rather than share how worried we were each really feeling, imagining the worst.

'It's the old "do-si-do" dance we do and have done over the years, isn't it?' I say. 'We seem to each turn inwards rather than towards each other and God, when there is trouble and stress and pain.'

'I know,' Kim agrees. 'I know my fall-back position is to suppress pain, push it down, pretend everything is all right. And not to share it with you, or indeed anyone else either.'

It feels silly when expressed aloud to each other now.

'It reminds me of that phrase your mother told me you used to say when you were young – "You're talking about something I don't want to think about."'

He nods. 'That's exactly how it feels when things are not going well. Why do we do this?'

Is it a fear of being thought a failure? Thinking others will judge us for not being 'shining lights of Christ's love' even when things are tough?

Or is it the traditional upbringing of tough boarding school for Kim and strict conservative evangelicalism for me? In neither place could one admit to emotions, to fears and failures, to not being the best one was supposed to be. Maybe we learned to be like this and now have to unlearn it, to be free of it in order to grow closer to one another. You'd think that after all these years we would have discovered this before.

I remember a poster my mother used to have in her kitchen. It depicted a Dalmatian puppy who looked rather guilty. Underneath was written: *Please be patient with me – God hasn't finished with me yet.*

Thinking of my mother brings back other stresses.

An Out-of-control Car

The situation in the north-London parish was not helped by a totally unrelated incident, an accident involving my mother and me. We had had huge celebrations for her 90th birthday earlier in the year; she was fit and well, still living alone, driving the elderly to church (!) and enjoying a busy and active life. I had been to stay for a few days, and she drove me to Tonbridge station to catch the train back to London.

As we stood by the car to say farewell, an out-of-control car knocked her over, swept her away and then ran over her, as I watched from where it had hurled me. It was a truly terrible way for her life to be ended.

The insurance claims and the court case took a couple of years and it all caused me to suffer tremendous post-traumatic stress, exacerbated by the constant sirens passing the church and vicarage, giving me terrible flash-backs. The psychotherapist advised me to move; the bishop was sympathetic and did all he could to help us find a solution, even suggesting Kim could commute from Hertfordshire.

But Kim also needed to leave the church, although I didn't realise it at the time; and my need to move gave him the excuse of leaving the parish.

So we left, on Christmas Day. There was a family service at church that morning, after which we leaped into the car to drive away and spend the rest of the day with our family. As we were going out of the vicarage gate, we turned to look at each other and there was a huge sense of relief, of escape, of leaving the unhappiness behind.

At least, that's what I thought at the time.

Now, I remember and realise how supportive Kim had been during my mental anguish and depression, even though he was going through a tough time himself. And how paltry my gratitude to him.

We hold hands for a few yards, asking for forgiveness again over these new revelations, stealing a light kiss, smiling into each other's eyes again.

It feels good. It feels better. And it feels much easier to do this while walking together in the same direction.

Maybe we *will* find ourselves in France after all.

Looking for Coffee

I pass on the offer and availability of coffee when we spot a lovely looking café.

'It's far too early to stop for coffee,' I say. Later, we pause instead under a bridge and perch on a low wall. The arches of the bridge are covered with huge graffiti outlined in strident black; it's not the most salubrious of places to eat green apples, stuffed in my pocket at breakfast. Now, after walking for an hour and a half, all I can think of is sitting down and sipping a deliciously fragrant energy-giving cup of coffee. We have to stagger on until, half an hour later, there is a lock in a little village by a road bridge; several canal boats are moored as there is a *boulangerie* which serves coffee. Best of all, it has a loo!

But no ice cream.

KIM:

The people we share the path with are an interesting mixture. There are very serious French cyclists, who look as though they are training for the Tour de France. Then there are the holiday cyclists on upright bikes, with bells they tinkle at us, and who when we call, 'Bonjour,' reply, 'Hallo! Good morning!' and are obviously English. I particularly enjoyed the in-line roller-skater who was whizzing along with a lovely rhythm and at twice our speed.

There are tiny circular tables just for two, and we ease our packs off and rest for twenty minutes and watch the world and its boats and cars go by. The yellow-and-white boat moors in front of us; we exchange greetings with its sailors. The coffee is hot and strong, the croissants are delicious and life is good. My phone pings with a text message from my friends Sue and Dee who are walking the Pembrokeshire coastal path today. We swap photos of water and sun and happiness and I think how blessed we are with modern technology and the joy of being in touch with family and friends.

Heaving up my pack, I am sure someone has put a heavy stone in it during an unguarded moment; it feels twice as heavy as when I took it off. But, refreshed and revived, we continue onwards and the signs show we are walking along a cycle pathway. Athens 3780 km one way, Cadiz 1610 km the other. I post a photo of the signpost on social media: 'Anyone like to join us on a pilgrimage from one to the other?' I enquire.

'Meet you in Athens,' one friend writes in reply.

Soon, below us on the left, there is an open, flat expanse, a nature reserve with several groups of pale white horses. Kim is very taken with them.

'I wonder whether they are wild, like the horses of the Camargue?' he says, taking photos.

There are pale herons, too, rising at their leisure as they see us pass, to land again a few yards further on. They are elegant in flight, solitary when standing. And there are beautiful wild flowers – cranesbill, alyssum, large purple-flowered thistles, morning glories, and roses – overhanging garden walls alongside the canal path. It all comes to an abrupt end with the outskirts of Béziers, which are busy, but the main road and its rows of second-hand car showrooms are across the other side of the canal.

Vodka for Lunch

Time for lunch and Kim goes online to find a good recommendation for somewhere to stop that is not too far out of our way. It means crossing the canal at the next pedestrian bridge, and finding our way through cars and people; already it's a shock as it seems busy and noisy after the delights of the towpath. Relaxing for an hour, we sit at a little pavement café at the Quai du Porte Neuf, enjoying an *entrée* and a double espresso each. This walk is already fuelled by coffee.

Table water comes in re-used Grey Goose Vodka bottles; we drink our way through several and the empty vodka bottles mount up on the table. Opposite us on the other side of the canal is a tall, elegant house: the roof tiles are golden with a green geometric pattern; the rectangular open tower has an ornate staircase slanting upwards inside.

It's lovely sitting here, I think dreamily.

'Time to get going,' Kim says, his eye on the mileage and the clock.

We are stiff and there are several groans because our muscles have seized up as we try to stand up after the lengthy break. The packs seem even heavier than when we set off and the temperature rises to 78F as we reach the *écluses de Fonserannes,* a flight of nine staircase locks on the Canal du Midi. Built by Pierre-Paul Riquet during the reign of Louis IV between 1666 and 1681, the canal is one of the oldest still in use in Europe and is now a world Heritage UNESCO site. These particular *écluses,* locks, are an impressive feat of engineering, rising seventy-one feet over a distance of nine hundred and eighty feet, and I pause halfway up to enjoy the views back to Béziers, while Kim searches beside the locks in the cafés and touristy places for a decent ice cream. But there's only wrapped or sit-down-with-a-scoop-or-three, and we prefer to press onwards.

The First Temptation

The temperatures continue to rise in the afternoon sun as the clouds dissipate. The towpath crossed the canal at the bottom of the locks, and the water and the sun are now on our left, with the light reflecting up from the water at us. I am glad I brought sunglasses. The bamboo towering over us on our right offers no shade as the sun is on the left. There are flitters of butterflies, while visitors out for a Sunday-afternoon stroll pass us, or wave from the pleasure boats. Kim points to a sign on the railings, advertising boat trips along the canal.

'We could take the boat!' he says, 'and hop off a few miles further along!'

It's certainly tempting. But we are not giving in, not on our first day, and we persevere to the BnB. Although it said in the description that it's by the canal, we can see no way to reach it on the towpath. The canal ahead bends left and the undergrowth reveals no pathway, so we detour a long way around on the road – only to realise that the towpath had indeed continued along the canal and we could have reached it that way. Despite the frustration, we arrive by 3pm and are greatly relieved to see a sparkling swimming pool in the grounds. We are soon enjoying its peaceful cool water (the only time I give in to this particular temptation) and Madame Stephanie provides madeleines, cold drinks and scoops of pink ice cream which, although sadly not artisanal, are certainly very welcome. We are so hungry we devour the lot. Swifts bombard us as we doze on the sun loungers and we try to summon up the energy to go and unpack.

The long, walled private terrace in front of our bedroom provides a place to rig up the camping washing line and hang out all the clothes we've rinsed through while showering. It becomes our afternoon arrival ritual: trampling out the smelly (and later very muddy) walking outfits under our feet as we sluice off the day's dirt and dust, wringing them out and hanging them to dry wherever we can.

'It's a good thing we purchased this lightweight easy-dry clothing from REI,' I say, 'but I can't see any way to use the built-in clothes pegs on the washing line!'

My knight in shining armour can see exactly how it works, and hangs up all the dripping linens. We hope they will dry overnight as it's a warm evening.

Finding the Route

Kim has a blister and he hobbles down to dinner. Unusually, he eats only a baked Camembert while I indulge in a 380g *côte de veau*. I've walked 13.88 miles and feel I've earned it today. And then we head to bed. Early bedtime and an early rise are to become the norm for us for the next few weeks. It doesn't take much to coax us to sleep after the rigours of the first day.

Chapter Two
Finding Yorkshire in France

The alarm goes early because we want to beat the forecast afternoon rain, but it takes us an hour to wake, brew and slurp coffee, sort, pack, get dressed up in all the walking gear and struggle into our backpacks. So it's 8am before we set off in the hopes of finding breakfast in the next village of Columbiers. As so often happens, I'm a few paces behind Kim, and his blue lightweight towel, attached to the outside of his backpack, flaps towards me in the breeze. I take a photo of him and send it straight to the family on WhatsApp.

'EU flag or diplomatic mission?' our son texts back.

Striding along with morning hope, glorying in blue skies and sunshine, I suddenly stop in alarm.

'Look! LOOK,' I say, my voice rising in a terrified shriek.

We watch a two-foot long, grey-and-black marbled snake slither across the road and up the bank into the undergrowth. I take a photo as it disappears in fear of us.

Vines and poppies line the road; a mother duck and nine ducklings greet us as we walk into the village, its old blonde stone tower reflected in the blue canal. There's an artisanal craft market in the square, the *boulangerie/pâtisserie* is doing a roaring trade and we enjoy *deux petit cafés* and *deux vienoiseries* and buy two quiches for lunch, all for €8 in total. The €10 each for breakfast yesterday was indeed far too much to spend.

It's the only market we encounter in the entire Great Walk. So much for my vision of stopping to buy oozing French cheeses and delicious fresh fruits at little village markets for our lunches, as we never arrive anywhere on market day on the entire trip.

Kim wanders around the stalls and falls in love with a pale-sage spotty-fabric dachshund and wants to buy three and have them shipped home to the granddaughters. I'm not so fondly sentimental and don't want to stop for the hassle of persuading the stallholder to post them for us and certainly don't want anything extra to carry, so we head towards the Canal du Midi again as the skies cloud over.

The canal soon disappears into the long Malpas Tunnel, and then heads north in a loop following the contours of the land. We prefer the shorter route, over gently undulating but rather boring countryside. The path is a tarmac little back road, devoid of cars, past an enormous Britvic juice factory closed on Sundays, and then down in to the Capestang, a huge nature reserve. After the recent rains it is more of a swamp land, with rushes and reeds poking out of the water, dark trees looming on the distant horizon. It's full of birds calling and cooing; a cuckoo is loud and persistent and we realise how long it is since we heard a cuckoo at home. Herons, grebes, storks, egrets . . . and others whose names we don't know. Two little otters swim away from us, frogs and toads croak, and the sounds of a water-land amaze us. It's far from silent.

There is no-one else around and it feels surreal to be in the middle of all this grey water under a low grey sky as far as the eye can see. There are few trees, only the occasional tufts of bushes, and the pathway across the middle is a brown semi-dry sludge. It is traversed regularly by armies of ants, busily following each other in lines from one side to the other. Eventually the path sinks under water; we pick our way gingerly through the shallowest muddy water we can find, and barely avoid it going over our boots. We are very grateful for walking poles assisting our steps; it's a relief to get out at the other end still relatively dry and find a bench on which to perch to eat the *quiche à porter*: crisp light pastry filled with a rich savoury yellow egg custard holding little cubes of ham and flavoured with fresh parsley. Cheaper and tastier by far than any supermarket 'meal deal' at home. It's followed by the little individual squares of dark chocolate saved from the *boulangerie* cup of coffee.

Walking after lunch we talk again, more deeply than for some time. It's easier to share things when walking side by side, walking together, looking out together in the same direction. There's not the intensity of eyeball to eyeball, which I think men particularly find more difficult. It unnerves them. But now, striding out together with a common goal, it seems much easier to talk and to divulge more of what's deep in our hearts.

We talk of mindfulness, of having a 'memo to self', of living for today, and of how to choose to live well for the next twelve hours and not worry for tomorrow and beyond. We can choose to live in a certain way just for the next twelve hours; that seems eminently do-able and not too heavy. And so we choose to live in a way that makes it easier to share with each other to talk and to pray together. The pillar-box red poppies nod at us as we go on to talk of friends we've not seen or indeed may even have rebuffed over the past few years, as we clammed up through the pain and stress and misery. The vines are in full vibrant leaf as we clamber alongside them, laughing together at the relief of talking, the relief of a sandy track after tarmac. There is the beauty of the beginning of restoring friendship, the beauty of a field laced with poppies, daisies and lavatera; the relief of being nearly at our next bed and breakfast.

The Nasal Accent of South-west France

Arriving slightly earlier than the anticipated 2pm, we timidly knock on the vast oak double doors of a once grand but now faded pink house, approached through enormous, tall, wide-open ironwork gates. The front 'garden' is a tangled overgrown mound of upright trees and bushes but the semi-circular gravel driveway still sweeps up to the *Domaine*, although it now has old tractors and rusty farm implements strewn around. There's a wrought-iron balcony over the front door, grey shutters flung back against the walls, a climbing rose. Monsieur enthusiastically throws open the door.

'*Entrez, entrez*, come in!' he says, welcoming us as his large moustache bristles with greetings. I point to my mud-encrusted boots, intending to remove them before I enter. '*Non, non!*' He laughs. '*C'est à la compagne ici! Hein!* It's the countryside here!'

We trudge in behind him and meet small, portly Madame who hovers behind him, smiling and nodding at us.

'Beer?' he asks us. '*Café? L'eau?* Coffee? Some water?'

Kim opts for a cold beer and I ask for hot tea *sans lait*, without milk. I pronounce it 'sonn' – at least I think I do; but Mme replies with '*saanngggg*'. It's our first encounter with the accent of the *sud-ouest*, of *l'occitane*. Occitan, or the Langue d'Oc, is one of several Romance languages that evolved from vernacular Latin, and was the language of the songs of troubadours. It's still spoken across southern France, with regional dialects. We hear its nasal twang a lot as we travel across this area of France, especially in the first couple of weeks, and we have to get used to it before we can begin to try to understand what is being said. Wine at supper becomes '*du vannggg*', breakfast bread is '*du pannnggg*'. We are trying to speak French Without Tears, although Terence Rattigan's own experiences of learning French were more northern, as he was in Wimereux, near Boulogne.

We follow Monsieur though a dark, stone-flagged hallway. A tall grandfather clock ticks in the far corner and a very large dresser stacked with books and china and glasses looms through the darkness. On our left, a wide spiral stone staircase comes down to finish with a twist and a whorl of darkened oak banister. Our spacious room is on the next floor. Small grey tiles in a mosaic pattern completely cover the floor; mud is certainly no problem here. The high-ceilinged room was decorated perhaps some forty years ago, mostly in pink. There are long muslin curtains blowing gently at the vast open windows, a small flat double bed with tiny bright-pink square pillows, two bright-pink armchairs, and, through a doorway, a completely white-tiled shower room. It's all glorious faded French country charm. We snooze, relishing the promise of a dinner cooked by a local chef.

By early evening we are so hungry we could eat any and everything. We have to walk next door, through the farmyard, to the house of Sassia, *la cuisinière*, the cook. It proves to be a most convivial affair with the other two overnight guests joining us: Monsieur Salvatore, who has an Italian mother, a French father and who was born and brought up in Belgium, and his delightful Flemish wife. They live near Dax, but met years ago at Taizé, the Christian retreat house in France. Conversation over dinner is a mixture of English, French, Italian, hand gestures and nods. It works extremely well and we cover Brexit, theology, literature, walking. Sassia joins in, popping out to stir and steam and sizzle the dinner, drinking copiously from a glass replenished frequently from bottles of wine that are also offered to us all.

'I'm from Algeria,' Sassia says when we ask about her background, 'and I was brought up Muslim. My brozzer and I, we became Christians when we emigrate to La Belle France.'

'Where does your brother live now?' asks Monsieur Salvatore.

''E was assassinated in Narbonne.' Sassia turns away and she doesn't explain more, so no-one likes to ask when she moves quickly on. She points to the large black-and-white photo propped up on the sideboard. 'Zat ees my father.' He reminds me of Omar Sharif.

There are five absolutely delicious courses. We enjoy *magret de canard*, never guessing that it will prove to be just the first of many. We are crossing duck country, we discover later. Sassia's *magret*, duck breast, is cooked in honey and butter sauce; we wolf it greedily.

Eventually, it's time to go – we want to begin early again tomorrow. Kim says in his best French, 'It's time to go and take my wife up to bed – *Je doit prendre ma femme au lit.*'

This is greeted with enormous guffaws of laughter; he has apparently used some metaphor meaning a whole lot more; M. Salvatore gets up and shakes Kim's hands.

'*Bon courage!*' he says, crying with laughter. 'Good luck with that.'

I'm blushing as the joke is explained and we all bond again over shared laughter and fun.

Doggy Bags and Drawings

After our large evening meal, it's not surprising that I'm not very hungry next morning at breakfast. It's croissants and milky coffee, toasted brioche, bread and fig jam. Never a great lover of ordinary croissants, and longing for fruit, yoghurt, protein, I pass on the carbs. Mme is horrified at my small breakfast. She grabs a paper bag and fills it with everything that's left on the table – croissants, slices of bread, more slices of rather stale because untoasted brioche.

'For you,' she says in her broken English. 'You take.'

We are touched by their kindness – Monsieur refuses payment for the beer and tea, just as Mme Stephanie refused payment for the ice cream and madeleines yesterday.

'*Pouf! Ce n'est rien* – It's nothing,' they insist, 'it's for your pilgrimage.' We are awed at the generosity of these southern French. It is to be a recurring theme.

Kim had cramp at dinner last night; over breakfast, Mme Salvatore talks him through some diagrams she has found in a book upstairs and copied out for him – reflexology or acupuncture for easing the pain. She has drawn pages and pages and translated the notes into English for him. Such generosity of time and labour.

'You 'ave ze cramps?' Monsieur Jean Luis says to Kim. 'You drink ze tonic water as soon as the cramp pains begin.'

He and Madame sit with their guests over breakfast, and take time to talk and converse. The conversation soon turns to what it means to be European.

'Me, I'm Catalan, Basque, and then French,' Jean Luis describes his great-grandparents and grandparents. Mme nods.

'I also a mixture,' she says, 'but me, I am a European, a mixture, like a mongrel dog.' It's a more fluid approach, it seems, due to history and take-overs; kingdoms waxing and waning.

'So you're really Heinz 57!' I say.

It doesn't translate.

It's hard to get away from the chatter and the croissants, and it's 8.45am before we eventually leave.

'*Bonne marche*,' they keep telling us, 'have a good walk!' It's a beautiful morning, less humid than yesterday, and we stride up the hill to a village and down the other side, looking once more to join the Canal du Midi.

'Who are we really?' Kim says, wondering aloud. 'Talking last night at dinner and then again at breakfast, I get the impression that they seem on the whole to be happy as European rather than French. We're an island, so maybe that helps explain why we are isolationist, British, even just English or Welsh or Scots.'

I nod.

'Yes, but when you and I lived in the States, I felt I didn't belong to either place, Britain or America. Neither seemed to be my real home, even though I preferred the American Penelope to the English Penelope,' I say. 'The States brought out the best in myself, I always felt, because I didn't perceive others to be judging me in the way I think they do in the UK. Maybe I just didn't know how to read what people felt or what was implied in what they said!'

Kim brushes away a buzzing insect and we potter on, thinking about who we are and where we truly belong.

'But as Christians we believe our citizenship is heaven anyway,' he says.

I agree. 'Yes. That old song, "This world is not my home, I'm just a-passing through . . ." and maybe not feeling at home anywhere here is actually a Good Thing as it makes us think about belonging elsewhere, specifically in heaven. Keeping your eyes fixed on things above.' I trip over nothing in particular.

'I should fix your eyes on where you are walking for now,' Kim says, teasing me. But that's difficult when the countryside is so lovely. We are walking on the edge of the Minervois wine country; vineyards line our way on the left and up hillsides the other side of the canal. Often there are puddles and streams in between the rows of bright-green vines, and old twisted trunks stand in thick mud. It's been a wet spring.

> KIM:
> You will never be completely at home again because part of your heart will always be elsewhere. That is the price you pay for the richness of loving and knowing people in more than one place.

By mid-morning we're already halfway on today's journey and we've reached the gorgeous little town of Le Somail, with its old stone buildings perched beside the canal, a mediaeval bridge, and cyclists stopping to admire the view and drink coffee.

'Positively romping along,' encourages a friend via Facebook when I post the photo of our halfway mid-morning stop. We pause just before an old bridge to take photos of the house opposite. It is a long pale stone edifice, hemmed both sides with tall dark cypress trees. There are pretty light-blue shutters at the windows and pink roses climbing the walls. The whole scene is reflected charmingly in the canal waters and it's picture-postcard beautiful. Just beyond the bridge we stop at a waterside café and imbibe more coffee while enjoying the view. It's a gorgeous place to stop for a while.

Unfortunately for Kim, the café doesn't serve ice cream, and we nibble surreptitiously on leftover breakfast from the paper bag. Suddenly, stale brioche is rather delicious.

We watch a large royal-blue boat try to navigate through the old stone bridge on our right. The back of the boat gets stuck on the far side of the bridge and there is a lot of shouting and swearing both from the crew and from the people on top of the bridge watching the manoeuvres. Once it is released on to the canal again, the elegant boat becomes our pace-setter, as we soon catch up with it when it has to slow when the canal veers right on a bend. It's fun to walk alongside, waving to the elderly sixty-somethings on board who are sipping wine under the blue-and-white striped awning. Surrey bend, Middlesex bend – we are winning! Kim's days of rowing at Cambridge and sweating along the Boat Race course on the Thames give meaning to the bends.

Oh wait – we're sixty-something too. Our pace quickens to ensure we don't look as old, and when we have to cross over the canal, we pause on the bridge and watch them go underneath us; but we soon overtake them again and head to Ventenac-en-Minervois for a lunch break. But alas: it's Monday and nothing is open and there's no *boulangerie* and certainly no artisanal ice cream. We're glad of the last few slices of brioche still in the paper bag, but I am longing for some fruit.

Retracing our steps to the bridge at the edge of town, we take ownership of a circular concrete picnic table and its benches for a rest, where we are serenaded by the village loudspeaker system, advertising boat trips on the canal. Kim rests his head on his backpack for a siesta, and as he does so, a strimmer starts up nearby. He snorts with frustration.

'Typical! Just as I'm snoozing – and it's echoing back at me from under this stone bench.'

The strimmer is continuous and annoying so he sits up. Realisation dawns: the 'strimmer' is in his backpack. He digs around and comes up with the electric toothbrush he has inadvertently turned on by lying on it.

> KIM:
> One of the things Penelope has to endure is my awful puns. Crossing the fast-flowing Aude I suggest that I should write an ode to the Aude. You have to read that aloud to appreciate it.

Rosy Rosé

We are cheered by the thought that we are 10 per cent of the way to the Atlantic, but we have to make a decision about the afternoon's route: 2 km by road, with the swishing cars whose drivers make no allowance for walkers, or 5 km along the canal as it makes a large loop and crosses an aqueduct.

'I think I'd rather go along the canal,' I say and we set off, but very soon Kim spots a shortcut on the map. Like most of his shortcuts in family history, there turns out to be a snag once we are too far along it to turn back. This one is a very steep hill in between rows of vines, up to Paraza. We sweat our way up in the heat of the early afternoon sun, and I wonder what else I should have omitted from my belongings to lighten my load. Kim is longing for a cold ice cream; the sun is intense and we are too early to arrive at the night's lodgings. But the only place open is the vineyard *Domaine*, offering *dégustation*, wine tasting. We've been walking through the vineyards of the Minervois, and one of the memories from Miles Moreland's inspirational book was his suggestion that the chilled rosé was the best and only wine to savour in this area. So we slip into the cool interior of the enormous converted old stone barn, gulp down ice-cold water in between sips of different chilled rosés and congratulate ourselves on another successful day. And buy a chilled bottle of 'Bad Rosy Rosé' for later. It just fits into the tiny cool bag I carry at the top of my pack. Cheers!

The route takes us through the hill-top village of lightly coloured stone houses covered with wisteria and climbing roses, and out the other side and then a steep descent back down to the level of the canal, which has come round the loop and rejoined us. Our destination is a house at canal level and it is at the end of a steep gravelled driveway that twists and turns its way down the hill between tall bamboo and grasses and trees. The house is a long, low, modern building, with a pool to the right-hand side. A glass front door in the middle is wide open and we call into the cool interior. Again it is the Monsieur who comes to greet us and he leads us left through the modern steel kitchen, across the dining room with a long red-baize-covered table, and out on to the shady terrace at the back of the house, the garden sloping down below us.

On the daily arrival at a BnB, we long to shower and change and relax, but as so often happens, our hosts are gracious and welcoming and want to sit and chat and press us to partake of welcoming nibbles. Madame now arrives – she is tall and dignified, with sweeping white hair lifted off her face; she is also German, so we are presented with generous slices of home-made German almond cake and some sparkling white Riesling wine, and long descriptions of why she and her husband left their farm in Germany to settle here. Kim is eyeing the pool longingly; I'm beginning to feel the effects of *dégustation* followed by bubbles. Eventually we manage to ask for our room, and there is time to stamp out the clothes and hang them on the proper washing line in the garden, before Herr Karl cooks us an amazing dinner. Devils on horseback; chilled carrot and orange soup, served with the tiniest scoop of ice cream floating in the middle; a rich turkey and hare casserole with herb dumplings; fruit compote and fresh raspberry mousse. There is no way I will shed any pounds on this walk through France. And it wasn't quite the way Kim has dreamed of consuming ice cream. But it is a simply delicious meal and we devour it all.

Herr Karl has cooked and served the meal to us, and while we eat Frau Karl sits and chats to us again, although she doesn't eat anything. The conversation is fascinating. Politics; a biography she has recently read about Yehudi Menuhin – she kindly emails me the title and author a few days later; and the details of their ecological farm near Dusseldorf and the incompatibility of the French culture as far as they are concerned.

'These French workmen!' exclaims Herr Karl. 'They don't show up when they say they will. Tomorrow will do, they say. They are incompetent!' Frau Karl nods in agreement.

'We find it very difficult,' she says in her prettily accented English. 'The culture is so very different to what we are used to. We are deciding to sell if we can; we want to return to Germany. We thought our family would come south a lot for visits, too, but it's been only once a year. This life is not what we had thought it would be.'

Kim talks and talks and loves the thought-provoking interaction. Later, he thinks more about the European interchanges.

'This morning, everyone was happy to be European. Tonight there is a gulf fixed between the French and the German. Interesting!' He is fascinated by political thoughts and situations. And I ponder more about Herr Karl's sadness about his life not being what he had thought it would be.

Is my life what I had thought it would be? Yet again, I am profoundly grateful for all that I have, for my good health and ability to do this walk, even at my great age! For my home and my family, for all that God has blessed me with. Being grateful has such a profound effect upon my mind, puts things into a better perspective; but it's a definite choice for me – my fallback position so often is negativity, comparison with others who seem to have so much more. Being grateful for what I already have includes a loving husband; daily being thankful for him rather than seeing the negative, and grumbling, has recently had a profound effect on our marriage. It's a lesson I have had to learn more than once in our married life.

A satisfying breakfast at last – protein! Our German hosts provide ham, yoghurt, cheese and fresh fruit as well as the ubiquitous French baguette and jams. We are on our way again by 8am, as planned, taking the 'short cut' recommended by Frau Karl as the best way to rejoin the Canal du Midi: behind the house and across two fields, past the tall bamboo and up to the towpath again. I think we take a wrong turning across the field somewhere because we are soon fighting our way through thick, tall bamboo and long grass.

Determined not to turn back, we leap a final ditch (no easy feat with heavy backpacks) and eventually find ourselves on the towpath. An hour later, in good spirits in cool temperatures, we stop at another *écluse* at Argens-Minervois. We sit outside in the pale morning sun, at a little round table, drinking coffee and watching a tourist boat growing higher in the lock with its occupants all sitting on the top deck eating a cooked breakfast as they rise. It seems slightly incongruous! The café sells packaged ice creams but Kim is still determined to find artisanal 'real' ice cream.

> KIM:
> The heat and the walking are causing our hands to swell. Penelope has developed a form of exercise using her walking pole, which she holds above her head and then she bends her upper body from side to side. It's very impressive to watch as she strides ahead of me, waving , twisting, bending.

Beating the Storm

When the canal makes yet another wide loop to the north, avoiding having to construct locks, we head straight on, braving another boring little back road. The temperature rises, the humidity descends, and my sinuses decide they are allergic to something. I swallow an antihistamine but feel lethargic and listless. I want to go home. I don't want to take another step. Whose idea was it to cross France on foot?

Kim tries to encourage me.

'You're just feeling a bit Day Four-ish,' he says, and has to chivvy me along to reach the next little village, Escales. I think I'm lacking sleep – last night was a disturbed night after the heavy rich dinner. He buys ice-cool water at the village shop, while I lie inelegantly on the wide ledge by the fountain in the war memorial square and do 'dead bugs' to ease my aching back. In public! And then discover that not only has my husband quietly returned but he has taken a photo of my inelegant position and, what's more, posted it on Facebook. I'm outwardly horrified but secretly laughing because I suddenly realise I really don't care anymore what anyone thinks. I'm just proud to be doing this walk!

I re-apply my lipstick to maintain some sense of decorum. It's futile; I am learning that there are things one just has to do on this type of walk. That includes squatting by the roadside if needs must. If I face away from the traffic I can't see the cars. So if I can't see them, they can't see me, I reason. It's the only way to achieve relief sometimes in a worst-case scenario.

This village boasts a glorious Norman-esque church, but for us the best facility is the public WC. It's fairly basic but it works; I'm learning not to be too fussy.

But there's no ice cream.

Suddenly the public tannoy system bursts into life, warning of impending *orageuses* from 2–7pm – thunderstorms and heavy rain coming very soon. There's still ten miles to go and the rain is due to arrive in two hours and ten minutes! We pack up and hurry on, hoping to arrive before the rain descends. The path is now very enjoyable, as we walk through a little pine forest with soft pine-straw under foot, and rosemary and lavender fragrance the air as we brush past the scrubby bushes. My spirits rise and I am enjoying the herbs, the fragrances, the soft pathway, the beauty around me.

The path is part stone, part rock, part earth, with confusing coloured flashes of paint ostensibly to show the way. As there are so many different colours, with so many different potential routes to take, we ignore them all and follow the route on Kim's iPhone. Another up-and-over-and-down, walking as quickly as we can to outrun the rain, but eventually we need to rest. We are on a three-stop strategy today but there's no bench in Roquecoubre-Minervois so we simply perch on a large stone by the roadside. It's not how I was brought up! Standards are definitely slipping. I renew my lipstick, and touch the pearls at my neck – there has to be *something* to help me remain civilised.

Or am I still assuming I am being defined by the outward appearance?

Next imponderable: keep going, or stop for lunch as we're tired and hungry, but then risk the rain descending? There are large black clouds threatening on the horizon but hunger and tiredness win; we check Trip Advisor and head towards a family run bistro on the edge of town. The *formule* or set menu is €12 for *plat* and *dessert*; soon a rich, fragrant ratatouille under a thick cheese crust is in front of us, accompanied by the best *frites* and some rather chewy grilled beef. I pass my meat to Kim and enjoy the rest. Alas, *glaces artisanale* despite being mentioned on the menu and on Trip Advisor, is off today. Kim is thwarted yet again in the search for proper ice cream. But the three-stop strategy seems to be working and we are re-energised and raring to go. Not.

The Canal du Midi comes around to join us and we pound along what is now a tarmac towpath. The balls of our feet are on fire, having been mostly on roads and pavements since mid-morning, the storm clouds draw ever nearer causing the humidity to rise even further, and our clothes are dripping and sweaty. The path is overhung with trees: willows and plane and bamboo; the grassy edge of the path is tall and overgrown. The canal is empty of boats here; it feels as though it's just the two of us in a rain forest, on a never-ending track. Or the Apocalypse has occurred and we are Left Behind. There's still a couple of miles to reach the village with tonight's accommodation – or at least, the signpost tells us it's still a few kilometres; but of course our beds may be the far side of town. We try to urge each other on.

French Siesta

Eventually the canal path comes out of the grassy green miles and begins to rise; there are some locks, and as we ascend the bank beside the first one at Puichéric, we see not only a signpost pointing across the canal to the two-star hotel but also the canalside back gate of the hotel. Nearly crying with relief, we cross over the bridge and haul ourselves up the steep garden path as it winds through rockeries and lush flowerbeds all decorated with metallic sculptures of fanciful designs. We reach the back door at exactly 4pm. Dropping his pack by the tables and chairs on the terrace, Kim strides confidently up to the door – but it is firmly closed. He rings the bell, knocks, rings again. There is a deathly silence.

'I did tell them in my email we'd be here between 3.30 and 4.30pm,' he grumbles tiredly. He tries again, then calls the hotel on his phone. There is no answer.

'How strange!' I say. 'Surely a hotel is open, especially now it's after 4pm. I wonder where they all are?'

A slight movement catches my eye – an open upstairs window is softly closed and I watch, amazed that someone is at home but not answering. They obviously don't want to hear our conversation. By now, I'm desperate for the loo, so I venture through the car park and around to the front door on the main road. It, too, is firmly locked – and there is a prominent handwritten notice exhorting me to note well that the establishment is closed daily from 2–5pm. We sink exhaustedly on to the terrace chairs, watching the dark clouds, praying it doesn't pour with rain just yet. I think I might just have to hide myself in the garden bushes for a moment . . .

At 4.35pm the back door is suddenly opened and a slightly faded, careworn woman appears.

'We work long hours,' she says. 'We have to rest and sleep each afternoon. *Alors*, why didn't you sleep on the sun loungers at the bottom of the garden?'

We are too tired to try to explain in French that we couldn't move another step and are too exhausted to walk back down the garden again, even for a sun lounger. And then back up again. We are both weary, frustrated, and perhaps even cross that we haven't been able to crash out as soon as we arrived.

Kim wonders *sotto voce* why she hadn't told him in her email of confirmation, not to arrive until 5pm.

Never mind; we are here and we are in. The relief is huge. And we can understand that they need their rest too. It's not easy running an establishment like this, I'm sure. *'Give me patience, Lord, to understand how life is for others, too,'* I think. My air of judgementalism fades and I remember again the phrase I am trying to live out: be gentle with others for everyone is carrying a burden you may know nothing about. It's certainly true for me and I am learning how true it is for others as well. I'm just a slow learner on this journey.

As soon as we reach our room, we forgive her for not letting us in sooner, for there is an electric kettle and two mugs in the basic but clean little room. I dive into my pack for Lapsang Souchong tea bags, and suddenly life is moderately civilised again.

The storm finally breaks at 6.45pm: thunder, lightening, torrential rain. Forget walking to the Trip Advisor-recommended bistro in town; supper will be at the little bar downstairs. I'm asleep by 9.30pm.

Yorkshire Tea

Next morning, fuelled only by the instant coffee provided in the room, we set out just before 8am in damp, grey mizzle. Breakfasts in hotels and guesthouses are expensive for what they are, we have decided, and we stagger into town along the ridges of the verge, trying to keep out of the way of the cars which speed past and catch the puddles and threaten a deluge over us. We're hoping for decent coffee and something to eat. At the first bar, we step inside and ask for *deux p'tit cafés*. As the tall young man who is serving behind the bar turns to the coffee machine, I notice a vast box of Yorkshire Tea bags on the shelf.

'They serve strong tea here,' I say in English to Kim.

'Aye oop,' or words to that effect, replies the young man in broad Yorkshire. 'Always bring it back wi' me when I take a trip to England.'

He explains how his parents bought an old farm not far away from here when he 'were nobbut a lad', and how every weekend they drove all the way from Yorkshire, worked on the house, and drove back again, until the house was ready for occupation, and then they moved permanently to France. He had tried working in England once, just a few years ago, when he'd finished school, hated it, and moved back to France and bought this bar. He looks about 19 and we find his Yorkshire accent almost harder to comprehend than the local French twang. His French is obviously fluent as he chats with other customers, but he has retained his accent of birth.

'You go 'n' get yerselves some breakfast *vienoiserie* over at that there *boulangerie*,' he says, 'an' I'll have yer coffee ready when yer gets back.' Or words to that effect!

His strong coffee keeps us going until mid-morning, when we reach Trebes. There is a 'boat jam'. Five boats are queuing for the thirty-minute passage through the locks, but only three boats can proceed at any one time. The ones at the back of the queue will be waiting for hours – the ones below have to come up, then the front ones go down, and then the next ones below have to come up.

'That would drive me insane,' I say. 'There's no way that's restful, sitting waiting for hours with nothing to do, getting frustrated at how long it takes, hanging around,' and I increase the pace, to prove my point: it's quicker to walk than go by canal boat. Kim grins at my impatience.

'So you don't want to come with some friends and cruise the Canal du Midi?' he enquires.

I assure him I've changed my mind on that one. And I remind him of the only time we've ever had a holiday on a canal boat. It was in the first year of our marriage and we went with some friends to cruise around the Cheshire Ring. In the end, frustrated with the terrible slowness of the boat and the same-ness of the riverbank, I deserted the boat and strode off across the fields to visit a stately house, rejoining the party easily after several hours away. At least I felt I had had some exercise and actually done something. And of course the canal was looping around in a ring, so my walk wasn't actually overlong.

'I know – I've always been too quick and too impatient,' I confess. I know I'm impatient with myself and with others; I like to get things done and get them done immediately, quickly, right now. And woe betide anyone who doesn't keep up with my fast pace. 'Lord, change me,' I silently plead. 'Give me your peace and patience and gentleness.' This Walk is reminding me and teaching me of so much. 'I'm really sorry about my impatience,' I say to Kim.

'You're just like your father,' says Kim, but with a twinkle in his eye.

German Shepherd Dogs

We sit by a cool, grey canal on a cool, grey day, and as we sip our espressos (best way to insert the caffeine) Kim checks today's mileage again.

'We've done ten kilometres so far,' he says. 'I'd worked out that today would be over twenty-four kilometres, but if we leave the canal and go up and over the middle it would save us about six kilometres. What do you think?'

I hesitate. We've already had one of his 'short cuts' and I know them of old. But the canal is getting persistent in its sameness and we are bored with it; it's done us well, initiating us into this long-distance walking on mostly flat paths, apart from our short cuts and deviations, but we might be relieved to bid it a fond farewell.

'All right,' I say, agreeing with a little reluctance. So we cross a full-flowing sludge-coloured Aude River and head out of town to dive down a little footpath, marked on the online map, and then follow it around the edge of a field.

A ferocious looking and barking German Shepherd dog leaps out of the trees and hedges ahead of us, snarling and baring its teeth and hurling itself towards us. I think I scream. We are both shaking with fright.

'NON NON NON!' Kim shouts at it. I hold my walking pole in front of me to ward it off. 'Contrôlez votre chien! Control your dog!' he yells.

No-one appears or answers. We try to walk faster across the muddy field but we are clogged down and our boots are heavy. The dog continues to circle us, still barking and snarling and lunging at us, stopped only by our poles. It runs at us again.

'Help, Lord,' I cry inwardly. 'Please protect us. Help!'

We break into as much of a run as we can with loaded backpacks and claggy boots, and Kim points to the steep grassy bank just ahead of us.

'Up there!' he gasps.

'I can't!' I moan, panting and sweating as much from fear as effort.

The dog continues its savage dance but holds back a little as we reach the bank. We can hear it snarling as we climb, grasping on to anything we can to gain a hold, gradually ascending, trying not to look back at it. The bank is short but it appears nearly vertical and heavy packs seem to drag us back. Reaching the 'summit' feels like a miracle. We find a stony track at the top, and we turn left and almost run along it, glad to be away from the dog.

The track turns a corner, we are into a farmyard and then – a stony grey courtyard with not one but *two* large fierce German Shepherd dogs, and they also begin to bark as they set out to charge us. But this time there are also two rather fierce-looking dishevelled men, who hurl abuse at us but call the dogs to heel. We cross the courtyard despite their shouts; there is absolutely no way we are turning round and going back the way we came. We head under the archway and out on to the main road.

'Oh my!' gasps Kim. We lean against the wall, shaking and trembling. Both of us are scared and frightened, emotionally exhausted. 'I need chocolate!' he pleads – I have it in my backpack.

'Let's wait 'til we get away from here,' I say. 'I'm worried they might still come after us!'

We find the next footpath and put as much distance as we can between us and the dogs and their owners, before we stop and slowly eat some chocolate, relishing the small burst of sugar and sweetness, calming ourselves. As we pause, we thank God aloud for his protection, giving thanks for safety in the first real danger we have had.

Lost in a Wood

Kim checks the online map again, and off we go, confident that we are now fine and will reach Carcassonne in time for lunch. The marked route on the map takes us up a small track, past an isolated house, then around the top of a field and into an area dense with broom, and with grass and boulders underfoot. But it isn't long before we are totally lost: for the first time, we are really and truly and properly lost. The path has disappeared, in spite of being marked on the map. We tramp around fields, crushing thyme and fennel and tiny cornflowers under foot; we push through scented broom and into thick trees and undergrowth.

It's the second scary moment this morning and again it's exhausting, physically and emotionally.

'This can't be right,' I say. I'm out of breath and worried, but Kim obstinately points to the marked path on the map. He is determined we are not retracing our steps, and so we battle on round another field and then into more trees. The low branches catch on our backpacks, bang into our faces, get caught on straps. I am terrified there are snakes or other nasties under the large stones, many of which are moss-covered and look as though they came from tumbled-down old buildings.

Eventually we see a narrow opening into some more thick trees, which might, just might, be a footpath. It is exceedingly overgrown, but it does indeed turn out to be a small track, and takes us over the hill and out of the trees. A whole hour to do just 2 kilometres. We emerge on to a broad path with views down a long tree-filled valley, just as the rains descend. I open my umbrella, a tiny telescopic one, but it gives some protection. It is to prove to be one of the best 'extras' that I've packed. We don waterproofs, tie the protective coverings over our backpacks, and try to summon up the energy to continue. Kim, I can tell, is exhausted, both by the dogs and by the trailblazing. He needs his engine stoking, but there's nowhere to sit and nowhere out of the rain.

At last, we perch by some modern houses, on a low wooden railing under a tree, and eat the toasted but now cold ham and cheese *Croques Monsieur* we purchased at breakfast time, along with a banana each and more chocolate. It's hardly a balanced diet, but there's also coffee. Flasks are the other 'extras' we are glad to have packed. Filling them at breakfast isn't always possible, but this morning's instant coffee is welcome. It's hot and reviving, especially with several sachets of sugar dissolved in its black depths.

It's hard to get going again. We are both tired, our muscles groan as we try to stand, and as usual the packs seem to have increased in weight over lunchtime in spite of our having removed lunch and emptied the flasks. But we have to get to our beds! We stagger on, in the rain and the mist, climbing up through a little town that, like so many French places, seems totally uninhabited, with the shutters closed and no-one around. Then, cresting a slight rise, Kim points ahead.

'There – look, LOOK!' he says to me.

Carcassonne

Turrets and towers and big thick walls are faintly discernible through the rain and the mist. The old *Cité* of Carcassonne is almost visible on the horizon. It looks like a palace from The Sleeping Beauty, its towers and turrets rising up from the mist and rain. It is an enormously satisfying sight, even though there's a little way to go yet. Eschewing the direct route on the main road as there is no pavement, we wind through the dismal modern suburbs, then along a muddy track and eventually come out opposite the old *Porte Narbonnaise*, the Gate from Narbonne, at the top of the *Cité*. We've made it, coming along the *route Narbonnaise*, just as the inhabitants of Narbonne would have done centuries ago.

But we are not being tourists today. And there's still quite a trek down past the old *Cité*, and over the Old Bridge to cross a river in full spate. We pause on the bridge to look back and then to take photos with the walls and ramparts up behind us, and are horrified at the sight! Someone has stuck or painted enormous yellow circles over the ancient grey ruins of the *Cité*. It's been spoiled and desecrated. Sacrilege! At least it matches Kim's grey-and-yellow jacket. Later, we discover it is a modern art installation celebrating twenty-five years since mediaeval Carcassonne became a UNESCO world heritage site.

We head on into the 'new' town to find tonight's BnB. It's a glorious townhouse, with views towards *La Cité*. Kim rings the bell and stands back as the door opens.

'Bon jour!' he says, summoning up conversational French.

'Aye oop – welcome, come on in!' or similar, comes back in more broad Yorkshire!

Finding a Launderette

Tomorrow is our first 'rest day' and we have two nights here. For the first time since leaving home, I unpack every single item from my backpack and spread it out to air. It feels almost voluptuous. We decide what to take to the launderette (everything except the clothes we don after a quick shower) and head out. Our hostess has assured us that there is a good launderette just around the corner. There is, but it's out of order. Lugging the laundry bag, which is heavy with all our wet muddy clothing, we trudge to the Tourist Office. Fortunately we were in Carcassonne some eight months ago and have a vague idea of the geography of the town. The Tourist Officer tries her best to locate another launderette but with no success, so we retire to the main square of the old *bastide* or fortified town, and sit under an awning which drips with rain. We drown our sorrows – Kim has a beer and, oh joy and at last, a decent artisanal ice cream. It's large, thick and creamy, just as he likes it. I opt for a kir royale, sparkling white wine laced with *crème de cassis*, the lovely blackcurrant liqueur. We try Google and online maps but can't locate another launderette.

It's time to regroup and plan the evening.

'I vote that on the way back we try the launderette again just in case it's been fixed,' Kim says, always the optimist, 'and then, while the washing is doing, we can we find some supper to have in our room.' He's feeling in much better spirits, fortified by the delicious ice cream.

As usual, he is right. The mechanic is indeed at the launderette mending it, and gets our machine going for us. Nearby, in wonderful local artisanal shops, we find chocolates, a wonderful quiche, fresh fruit (in that order!) and stagger along with the washing and the food, wishing we'd thought to bring one of the backpacks; at the time of leaving the house, it was just a relief not to have to wear one.

Taking the damp washing home, we drape it around the little suite – we have a bedroom, a sitting room and a large bathroom in this gorgeous house. And a balcony with a view of the river and *La Cité*. It's a treat for our rest day. Downstairs on the main floor, the management provides cutlery and crockery to eat supper, plus an honesty bar with bottles of excellent wine and coffee. While Matt is finding us plates and some decaf coffee for the cafetière, we chat with Rose. They are young hosts with a two-year-old daughter.

'We come from Saltaire in Yorkshire,' she says and we exclaim excitedly.

'It's where we spent the first year of our married life,' I tell her, and it's nice to have a connection. It's also good to be reminded of those heady, happy days of early married life, as we try now to rebuild a broken relationship.

'We wanted better weather, a better life, a larger house,' Rose says. They've emigrated to a new life in Carcassonne, and live in the basement flat of this gorgeous townhouse while doing BnB upstairs, and Matt, a therapist and counsellor, commutes to wherever he is lecturing, or sees his clients online. They are flourishing. So are her parents who are also staying for their regular visit.

But here's another element of the European question – what will happen to British immigrants after Brexit?

'I'm fine,' says Matt, 'because I'm originally from Eire and I have an Irish passport. And our daughter is fine – she was born in Carcassonne.'

'So what about you, Rose?' I ask. 'What might Brexit mean for you?'

'We're seriously considering becoming French citizens,' she says, 'but I might also try to get an Irish passport.'

What will Brexit mean for all of us who are Europeans? And *are* we Europeans? Or are we English, Yorkshire, Irish, French? We chat on, discussing politics and commuting and walking. It is perhaps a relief to talk in English; but we miss our usual nightly Franglais.

We retire to our suite, which is decorated in dusky blues and greys, highlighted with gold, and filled with a French *armoire* and other delightful antique French furniture. The rooms are all beautifully restored and furnished to a high degree of luxury and I award Kim 5 stars for his choice of accommodation on this occasion. It is deliciously comfortable and feels decadent after some of the rooms of the past few days.

The afternoon's perambulations for launderette-hunting have added an extra 3 miles to today's total. The good news is that there was a delicious pile of parcels awaiting our arrival. We now each have a pair of gel insoles for our boots, to swap around and give our feet a change of pressure, and I have a sleeveless walking shirt. And the house-sitters at home have forwarded the walking socks Kim had ordered but which hadn't arrived by the time we left. The wonders of modern technology and modern postal systems make us extraordinarily thankful. We are blessed.

And breathe . . .

The First Rest Day

Rest Day. And we (perhaps that should read I) want to explore *La Cité*, the old mediaeval fortified town on top of the hill.

'Don't you ever rest? i.e. SIT DOWN?' enquires a friend via Facebook when we post the day's adventures later. Not today – I want to see it all. But Kim has a large and painful blister and it's not responding to our usual treatments. Rose calls her doctor and Kim hobbles off to the surgery, returning with vast pouches of medication to cleanse, treat, wrap, restore. We're grateful to be members of the EU and able to have free health insurance in Europe.

La Cité of Carcassonne dates back to Roman times, and was extended during the thirteenth and fourteenth centuries with huge battlements and towers and a double row of gigantic ramparts. Inside the portcullis was a whole town with shops and houses and a church (the Basilica), all built around the twelfth-century *Château Comtal*. By the nineteenth century it was in ruins and Napoleon wanted it destroyed completely, but the locals opposed that idea and Eugène Viollet-le-Duc was appointed to oversee the restoration work. It took fifty years, and used a lot of imagination! The authentic reconstruction/reproduction has made it look like a Disney-esque fairy tale. Its internal beauty is now somewhat marred with tourist shops and restaurants of rather mediocre worth – think cheap swords, chain mail and fridge magnets; or eating over-priced *cassoulet* served by wenches in mediaeval garb. But look above and beyond the ordinary and it's still enchanting.

We are there early enough to beat the hordes of Asian tourists and we tour the chateau in splendid isolation, remembering and imagining scenes from Kate Mosse's trilogy set within the walls. A few weeks before setting out on this Walk, I dragged Kim to a session at the Bath Literary Festival with Kate Mosse as the speaker, talking about Carcassonne, where she has a home and where her latest book is also set. After the talk, I asked her to sign my copy of the book and told her what we were about to do. 'Enjoy your walk, Penelope!' she wrote in the front for me.

When we were here eight months ago, we toured the 'new' town using the map in the back of one of her books to show where her characters lived and where some of the action had taken place. But Kim was not long out of his Achilles boot, walking had been slow and hard going, and he had then sat in a café while I did a whistle-stop tour of *La Cité*. Now we both want to explore it in more detail.

The sweeping views over the town below and across to the snow-capped Pyrenees are stunning. As the crowds begin to arrive within the walls, we head into the basilica, the old tall cathedral; it's still swathed in drapes to hide the restoration work going on inside, but the mediaeval stained-glass windows glow at the east end, and we sit and listen to an Orthodox choir singing in the transept. It's breathtakingly beautiful to look and to listen. One of those special moments when the world and all it entails recedes into dimness and this moment, this place, this sound, are all that matters. God is very near.

I close my eyes and for a moment or two I can just *be*. Nothing else matters except *be*ing here and now, surrounded by ethereal beauty of stone and glass and sound, feeling the presence of God in a way I usually find hard. It's not a physical closeness; just a sense that he is near, just as I know that he always is, but I don't normally stop for long enough to sense and know that. I suppose it's something I take for granted – Immanuel, God is with us.

Is this the art of living in the present moment? I'm not very good at slowing down in order to inhabit this moment, this time, in all its fullness, letting go of mental confusion and busy-ness and reacquainting myself with God's presence, with his nearness to me and my dearness to him, as someone once said.

I breathe deeply, a sigh, really, and sit back and relax and appreciate this moment, this place, this nearness. I could stay forever. *This* is what really matters.

Here might I stay . . .

How can I continue this at home, I wonder? I shelve the question for now, intending to think about it more deeply another time.

Down below *La Cité* and over the river is the *bastide*, or *La Ville Basse*, the lower town, set out in a rectangular grid. It's the 'new town' dating from the thirteenth century but destroyed when the English Black Prince set fire to it. That was during the Cathar Wars of Religion; a lot of the historical buildings now date back to the seventeenth and eighteenth centuries and are large and grand. We wander around and then head to a recommended lunch stop and enjoy a typical French leisurely lunch, for two and a half hours, savouring the food, watching the world go by. The table next to us has an older couple (actually, read the same age as we are) also enjoying their lunch. We nod and smile at one another. They are finished long before we are, and as they rise to leave, Kim realises that they have drunk only half of their *pichet de rosé*. He smiles and points; they laugh and nod and pass it to him. We all laugh. France is being so good to us!

Later, the town house beckons, and we do indeed rest, and have an afternoon to read and write and snooze and look at the ubiquitous rain. But we don't care – for now. For now, we have only to rest. And write a blog post about the first section of the Walk.

It's good to take a longer look back at the early days of this Walk Across France. We're covering thirteen to fourteen miles a day, and it feels great. There has been laughter – and tears; the fun of our broken French discussing Brexit and books and other banter with our hosts or other guests; the pain of stretched muscles, a blister, yet another day of rain and mud and uphill stretches. We have laughed a lot together – something that has become rare at home, and it feels good. We chat together but we can also walk in a good-feeling silence. And we tell ourselves, 'We can do this!' Passing boaters tell us, 'Be admired!' which, although an odd translation into English of their thoughts, feels good too. Of course, some people tell us we are slightly crazy and others obviously think we are – but that, in a strange way, feels good too.

The end of January, when our marriage was in tatters, after the stresses of the past years left us broken emotionally, spiritually and maritally, seems a distant dream – or nightmare. The separation feels impossible. Now, we are a team, working together to make this challenge work. It's reviving us, helping to restore and renew in an even stronger way. We are beginning to find ourselves in France, individually and together, remembering who we are, who we want to be, who we are made to be.

'It's never too late to be who you were meant to be.' Often assumed, probably wrongly, to be a quote from George Eliot, it reminds me that it isn't too late; that my future does not have to be determined by my past; and that I want to be daily transformed, changed, grown, to be more Christ-like in my daily life, in my marriage, in my soul.

And we all, with unveiled face, beholding the glory of the Lord, are being transformed into the same image from one degree of glory to another. For this comes from the Lord who is the Spirit. (2 Corinthians 3:18 ESV)

Chapter Three
Finding Ourselves on Pilgrimage

Although we are sad to be leaving beautiful Carcassonne, we are stepping out into the second week of walking and that feels amazing. Kim takes a while to treat his blister, Matt fills our flasks, Rose gives us doggy bags of pastries and bread, and poses on the doorstep for a photo with us. And it's suddenly 9.30am. We're late! But at least we are walking on the grassy level, beside the river. And, we discover, following the Camino de Santiago.

The temperature rises as another shortcut takes us through an area of suburban light industry. The tarmac is hot and heavy underfoot and I need a loo. There's no hedgerow to go behind, no turnings or trees. I am feeling rather desperate and very afraid. Past the car depot, the bottling factory, the storage units. Unending pavement and roads. And then – one of the most welcome sights seen so far: never have I been so glad to see the Golden Arches – a MacDonald's.

As we leave the suburbs and head out in the country at last, the snow-capped Pyrenees stretch along the horizon to our left, glistening in the sun. Standing on a modern bridge over a busy motorway, we gaze at the endless stream of traffic moving swiftly underneath us. Kim has one of his best ideas yet.

'I'm going home!' he says. 'I'll collect the car and we can drive to the Atlantic. It's only four and a half hours from here via the motorway.'

Dream on.

After lunch, a pilgrim stone sign tells us it's 1254 km to Compostela.

'I am so glad we are not going that far!' I say.

'True, but I still need some artisanal ice cream. And I bet you are wanting more coffee,' he says, laughing at me.

KIM:

As we set off, a couple called to us, '*Bonjour* – Compostela?' as if we were on route to Compostela on a pilgrimage. And we have just found that we are indeed on the *Chemin Pyrénées de St-Jacques de Compostelle*. We are actually following it today to Montreal. So, yes, today we are on pilgrimage. France is by now largely a post-Christian country, so it's interesting on this pilgrim route how many people have called out to us, '*Bon Camino!*' They think we are going to Compostela, and there is still a respect for the pilgrim.

Coming off the bridge, we turn right and stride on to a farm track crossing a flat plain with no shade; golden fields stretch out both sides of us. We've emptied the flasks either during the morning or after lunch, but there is still some way to go today. So we are both delighted to see a village marked on the map just a little way ahead.

'We can by-pass the village and keep going, or do a short detour to see if there is a café,' Kim says, offering options. 'Worth a slight detour perhaps?'

Bath Rugby

So we walk into the little village of Arzens, in the hope that there will be a café. There isn't, but there is a down-at-heel bar with an open door. An old snooker table and a slot machine lurch on the terrace alongside rusty tables and chairs.

'I'm not going in there,' I say hesitantly. 'It looks very suspicious and very seedy.'

It's certainly not the sort of place I would normally enter. Kim obligingly goes in to take a look around.

'It's all right,' he says, emerging without his backpack. 'They like rugby and they know about Bath.'

Rugby in general, and Bath rugby in particular, create a link between Kim and other men wherever we are in south-west France, and he is soon propping up the bar chatting in French about rugby to the sole customer, an ancient, large (gentle)man accompanied by his ancient large black dog; and the bartender, who is thin, tanned and bald on top with a long, grey ponytail. They discuss the relative merits of *le quinze* versus *le treize*, fifteen or thirteen a side. Kim and south-west France seem to prefer *le quinze* as far as I can make out. We have plenty of time – it's still only 2.30pm and tonight's hostess has asked us not to arrive until 5.30pm. So the rugby chat is long and enthusiastic. I order an *affogato*; it's not been heard of here, so I ask for an espresso, a vanilla ice – *une boule seulement, s'il vous plaît*, one scoop only, please, and an empty bowl, and create my own.

I walk to eat and eat to walk. At least, that's what I promise myself.

When we are clearly outstaying our welcome, we adjourn to the benches in the shade of the plane trees. Kim dozes through another lesson of French with Michel Thomas; I read another chapter of *Brideshead Revisited*. I've chosen it out of the many available on my Kindle as being a profound, lengthy old friend. It doesn't let me down and I'm soon engrossed. Much as I usually prefer 'real' books, I am hugely grateful for my Kindle on this trip, with over two hundred and fifty novels, three translations of the Bible, a dictionary, a prayer book, daily devotionals, and various other resources, all on this tiny device. I just have to remember to keep it charged. That's not normally a problem; we have very nifty little pouches containing dual chargers on French plugs, and I can charge the batteries on my phone and watch overnight and the Kindle during dinner.

But Kim has forgotten or mislaid one of his leads: it's for his iPad and he needs that recharged for our maps and the detailed information. So it gets first charge on my Kindle lead. He promises to order another lead online for delivery to our next two-night stay. The lack of a lead has become a bit of an issue between us, and I have to learn afresh that no-one's salvation is affected. 'Although your life might be at risk,' I say, growling at him. He tickles me and I have to laugh. No, the lead doesn't really matter and I need to learn what is, and what is not, worth making a fuss over. But I will be glad when the replacement arrives.

The pharmacy opposite our benches opens its doors at 3pm after the lunch break; I suggest Kim pops in as he needs a small toothpaste and I need a pocket-size pack of tissues. He comes back triumphantly bearing a large pack of not one but ten pocket-size packs of tissues.

'It was on offer,' he says. He loves a bargain. 'Five packs for each of us.'

All I can think of is the extra weight to carry. 'They will be very useful,' he assures me. I will remember that every few days, squatting by various roadsides or in the hedgerows. He was right as usual.

A Dream or a Nightmare?

The temperature gauge on my watch informs me it's 83F as we stagger along tiny little back roads, following the blue and gold Camino shell signs. The Black Mountains edge the right-hand horizon, the Pyrenees edge the left. Both are clearly visible; rain is forecast. As we march down a little village street in Montreal, trying to locate tonight's house, we pass a small grassy field on our right, between two houses. There is a rusty farmyard gate; three women are sitting at a dilapidated picnic bench, clearly and vociferously enjoying a bottle of wine. As we head on past it and down the hill, there is a shout.

'KEEM! KEEM!'

We pause and turn around to see one of the women running down the hill, long black hair streaming back from her face, and impeded by her bright floor-length skirts.

'*Je suis* Camille! KEEM! Come . . .'

I don't think they see many backpackers around here.

We are staying at *Les Rêves de Camille*, Camille's Dreams; and so far it is mostly a dream. Which becomes our nightmare.

'Excuse,' she says in her charmingly broken English, leading the way over tarmac and broken paving, into a still-concrete-floored living room. 'I here three months yet. Work still to do. Men don't come.'

And she goes on to explain that the workmen don't turn up as promised and the renovations have a long way to go and she finds it exceedingly frustrating working in the French culture where the workmen don't turn up when expected. The same story we hear several times.

Camille has moved here from Belgium, to fulfil her dream of a little house in the country. She worked in the Palais de Justice in Brussels, and is now wanting a new life for herself and hopes to fund it by living in south-west France and offering BnB.

'I don't think she bought the right house, though,' Kim says as he sniffs the damp. 'And there's hardly any water pressure in the shower and none of the doors close properly and the bathroom is still only half plastered.'

We decide to be polite and describe it as rustic; and as there are Earl Grey teabags and a kettle and mugs in our room, thoughtfully provided for 'Les Anglais,' we forgive the unfinished house. But Les Rêves de Camille have yet to materialise and the so-called double bed is really just a generous single; and for the first time, no pillows, just the traditional French round and solid bolster stretched across the top.

'But even this is more luxurious than the mediaeval pilgrim might have had,' I say to cheer us up. 'We do have a shower and we do have a bed, and we can make a cup of tea. It's not that bad really.' My standards are obviously slipping, and yet it's true: we are blessed to have comparatively so much.

We trudge back uphill through the village to find supper – a mile round trip to add to today's total. But the evening sun is warm and we eat outside on the terrace and realise that all the other tables are occupied by British couples. The table immediately next to ours has two married couples, obviously both from Yorkshire. Of course; where else would they be from?

We are soon all the greatest of friends and they explain that the couple on the far side have just today moved from Yorkshire into their new home in the village; and their friends, the nearer couple, have come to help them move in. And what are we doing? they ask, and we explain. As they get up to leave, the new householder slips Kim a €20 note.

'Put it in your sponsorship fund,' she says, patting his shoulder.

They drive off in an enormous open-topped mustard-coloured BMW. We wave them farewell and wish them all the best in their new home.

It's a long and sleepless night. Neither of us is comfortable, the bolster is hard, the bed narrow and too short for Kim's long legs. We rise early, glad to be out of the bed, and are soon packed and ready to go.

Onwards and Upwards

Saturday is another day. But it is to be a long day – tonight's hostess has stipulated not to arrive before 6pm so we walk slowly and that, we discover, is more tiring than striding along. Then comes a long, steep climb, our first really demanding one. We agree to go at our own pace. Kim likes to attack the hill, stretching out his long legs, stopping often to admire the views and taking a long well-earned rest at the top; he sets off again as soon as the laggers (that's me) catch up.

I, meanwhile, prefer to take it at a slow, steady pace, breathing regularly to some inwardly sung rhythmic song, bending the knees, not pausing until I reach the top. On past walks, I have struggled to keep up with Kim and felt inadequate when I've pushed myself to the limits, and suffered stabbing chest pains. Now, I'm independent enough to insist on doing it my way. It works much better, and we take time to be alone with our thoughts.

Keeping on keeping on can be tough. Finding ways to cope that mean we are able to keep going is important, yet it's taken us over forty years of marriage to work out how the other tackles the steep inclines and how we can do it differently and still survive. It's a good metaphor. Onwards and upwards.

There is a community café in the next village. It offers coffee for residents at €1.20 and at €1.50 for non-villagers. We have two each. We stay put in the comfortable armchairs for an hour; there's no rush today and as there is free Wi-Fi in the café it's a good place to stop and catch up with emails and news online. And there's good phone reception too. Kim decides to call tonight's hostess and ask if it might be possible to arrive a little earlier, maybe at 4pm. She talks faster than fast and he has difficulty understanding her nasal twang of the local accent, but he assures me that she says she will let us know when she has managed to have a friend meet us to let us in.

My iPhone is monitoring my mileage. It vibrates into life and informs me I have just completed the whole of my June challenge already, and it issues me with a picture of a trophy.

'Can I stop now?' I enquire, as it's only June 9th and I'm an award winner already. But we need to get to our accommodation so I plod on.

Sleeping in the Stables

The recent heavy thunderstorms have damaged the countryside. Maize is standing in water, the grass verges have slipped away, mud has slithered across the roads and paths. Fields are under water and the banks of road and river have beige mud stains going up several feet.

'I'm glad we didn't set out a week or two earlier, we would have been walking in those thunderstorms,' says Kim. 'At least we've had some sun – and, look, there's a good place for a picnic.'

We lie on the grass and doze in the hazy afternoon sunshine. I'm wearing the new sleeveless shirt and the sun is behind me. My head and shoulders begin to feel warm and I fall asleep for a few moments. I'm woken by Kim's voice. He's phoning Madame. It's a long conversation as he explains it's three o'clock and we are only an hour away.

'*Alors!* But if you had let me know, I could have had a friend let you in!' she cries.

'I don't think my French is so good after all,' Kim says to me in surprise. 'I thought we had already talked about that.'

We potter along until we are approaching the village and he tries to locate the exact whereabouts of the house on his map. He can't find it and there are two roads into the village. Which is going to be closest to the house? He phones Madame again.

'Are you north or south of the village?' he inquires.

'*Non, non* – come from the *autoroute!* It's only four kilometres from the exit,' she tells him.

He tries to explain that we are on foot, *au pied*, walking not driving. But she won't have it.

'*Non*, take the exit from the autoroute.' And not to arrive until 6pm.

Kim is by now convinced that she is one fry short of a Happy Meal; I silently think she must be fed up with these guests who keep pestering her on the phone while she is away from home.

For now, the only thing to do is find a bar or café and sit and wait. Dismally we wander up and down long roads of modern bungalow-type houses, squalid patches of abandoned cars and farm implements, tall hedges shielding other things from view. No café or bar emerges and the only place to sit is a stone bus shelter, full of rubbish, dead leaves and other unmentionables. It starts to drizzle. The flask is empty. My pack is heavy.

'No marks for tonight's accommodation either?' asks Kim. I grimace.

Eventually it's nearly 6pm and we manage to locate the house and wait some more, propped against a large stone wall on the driveway. It's nearly 6.30pm before Madame arrives at full speed in a tiny blue car, skidding up the hill that leads to her house and then on up to the equestrian centre that, we discover later, is beyond.

''Allo, 'allo!' she cries brightly, springing out of the car and continuing to jabber way in rapid French. It's high pitched, with the local twang; I struggle to understand very much of what she says at all. I am fascinated instead by her tight blonde curls bouncing up and down in time to her words. Madame is short and a little plump but she seems to spring on her toes the whole time, her curls dancing away. We gather that she is a shop assistant and works until 6pm but today had a customer who would not leave and who made her late. I feel even more guilty about our many phone calls.

We are ushered into the open-plan house and across the living area to a small bedroom which has a shower behind a curtain in one corner. The toilet is back across the main living room, by the front door, and I manage to get shut in – I just cannot get the door open again. I have visions of Kim having to break the door down. I can hear her offering a beer and him accepting; I wonder what I will do if I need the loo in the middle of the night.

Eventually, I rattle the door handle and Madame comes to let me out. I can tell that she thinks I am mad, as it seems to open very easily from her side. She shakes her curls at me.

'Don't shut the door!' she scolds me in her rapid French. 'When you are there, leave it a little open and it will not stick!'

Really?

We sit with Madame in her little outside courtyard, and the beer and the wine seem to relax the atmosphere. She explains that her house used to be part of the stables for the equestrian centre further up the hill, and she is gradually renovating it. But the workmen don't always turn up when they say they will.

'That explains the dampness and the horrible smell,' Kim says to me later. 'The aroma has not totally left!'

And then, to our amazement, Madame says that there is nowhere for us to have dinner locally and she doesn't cook, but she will take us in her car down to the Canal du Midi at Castelnaudary; that it isn't far to drive and there are several lovely restaurants by the water. We can phone her when we've finished and she will come and collect us again.

And so that is what she does and we sit by the canal at a waterside restaurant, and eat huge pots of *moules normandie* – mussels cooked with bacon, mushrooms and cream. Building our muscles. I lean back against the blue chair with a satisfied sigh. This is what I expected – eating *en plein aire*, in the twilight of a warm summer evening, enjoying good French cooking, glad to have completed another day's walking. There are narrow boats moored alongside, families laughing and chatting, busy waiters rushing in and out of the restaurant with plates of charcuterie, steaming fish, bottles of wine. I love this.

Madame collects us as promised as dusk is falling and we are grateful for her generous chauffeuring. But when we get back to her home there is another car parked outside. A tall man, introduced as *'mon ami'*, is sitting in front of the television, watching football.

Embarrassingly, the only way to the toilet from our room is directly between him and the television, and I can't shut the door properly or I'll be stuck, and the toilet is only just beyond him. I tell myself that I will never see him or her again and to just get on with it. After all, it could be worse – we could be mediaeval pilgrims camping out under a hedge.

Chapter Four
Finding Beauty in the Challenge

Breakfast is a sorry affair. Madame is morose and silent; the croissants are dry and small and pre-wrapped in cellophane; and the coffee is not good. As we get ready to depart, she asks for €5 each for breakfast. Kim is aghast.

'But I booked BnB – I thought the second b means breakfast!' he says to her. Guess it doesn't when you translate it into French. She insists on €10 so we turn out our pockets. Between us, we have a €20 note and a total of €8 in small change. Madame is not amused. She has no change for the note but she wants the full €10 and not just 8. Kim gives a Gallic shrug, places the €8 on the table and tells me we're leaving. She lets us out of the house without another word. We notice the other car is still there.

It's hard to pray blessings on her and her home after that, but we do because it's what we do every morning as we join hands and commit the day to the Lord and then ask for protection and strength. So we pray our morning prayer and as we do so our humour returns and we have to laugh about yet another experience in rural France.

Kim is not feeling his best, though, after another poor night's sleep, owing mostly to the bed having a foot board which meant he was uncomfortable. The odd position gave him cramp again and he is feeling slightly part-worn this morning. I can only commiserate and pray for him.

Scaling the Dragon's Back

The route today is not as long, but it is to be the most challenging day so far. After a few yards walking steeply up the main road out of the village, we cross over, duck through a gap in the hedge, traverse a field and are faced with what looks like a vertical green hill. The clouds are low and grey, the grass around us glistens with a luminous beauty after a heavy dew, and my backpack feels like a dead weight. Kim appears revitalised by the challenge of a tiny earth track leading him straight up; a few long strides, a huff and a puff and he is triumphantly on the summit and striding forwards. He disappears from sight.

I look hesitantly at the incline and acknowledge that I am actually slightly scared of trying to climb it. I look around, at the long grass surrounding me, the hedges, the hillsides and, already down below me, the road meandering along and climbing gently around the hill. Unless I return to the road and take the long way round, something we have already discounted as being too long, too monotonous and unadventurous, I am going to have to climb this hill. I bend forward, grasping at grasses and rocks, neither of which offer any help, inching up in a zig-zag, testing each step – and going so slowly that I am doomed to fail.

Soon, I'm stuck. I'm bent over, weighed down by my pack, terrified to risk trying to climb yet fearing a bad tumble back down the hillside.

It seems a while before Kim realises that he is alone on the top and returns to see what has happened to me.

'Just keep going,' he encourages me. 'It's not far now.'

I try, I really do, but it's no good. He descends a few steps, holds out his walking pole and as I grasp it, he pulls me up and I stagger on to the summit.

'Two people are better off than one, for they can help each other succeed. If one person falls, the other can reach out and help. But someone who falls alone is in real trouble.'
(Ecclesiastes 4:9–10 NLT)

We are meant to Do Life Together with others, in community, and that's especially true when things are tough. And this is tough: the summit shows not a lovely straight path along a ridge, but what I immediately call the 'dragon's back'. The ridges of this sleeping giant rise and fall ahead of us, some gently, some steeply. But I'm up the first one and although it promises to be a challenging walk for the next little while, there are stunning compensations.

At first, it's just the view, 360 degrees of glorious views, backlit with the sun's rays from behind the grey clouds. And as we climb, we can see further and further: rolling hills, green fields, forests. Only marred to our right by looking down on the 'corporation dust heap' or landfill site. Our eyes are soon filled with something else, however, as the lush grass is speckled with gorgeous wild flowers. It's not the carpets of poppies that we have so far seen; this is wildly, quietly, almost surreptitiously surprising us as we notice more and more – wild orchids, daisies and marguerites, yellows, purples, bronze, burgundy. And masses of tiny blue ones. Each bloom shyly peeps up from the longer green growth surrounding it.

Kim is enchanted with it, and especially because flitting between them are tiny delicate blue butterflies.

'It's almost as though the Good Lord painted the flowers, and then had some paint left over and thought, what am I going to do with this? I know, I'll paint some butterflies,' he says, standing to watch and look and take it all in.

There are plain white butterflies too, and white with black spots, and yellow ones; and black insects with red spots – we wish we knew their names, and yet it doesn't matter; we enjoy their glad fluttering on the gorgeous foliage and feel uplifted and grateful and glad, even though there is another steep little climb ahead. Taking time to stop and notice and be thankful restores me and I feel better able to tackle the next incline. Gratitude definitely helps with keeping on keeping on, looking for the beauty even when it's hidden and barely discernible. And it's definitely revitalising Kim, who now has a spring in his step and has forgotten the discomfort of the night.

KIM:
I was absolutely not feeling my best this morning. I was awake a lot of the night, with my feet sticking over the footboard and feeling very uncomfortable with burning sensations in my foot and thigh and both shins. I really wondered if I was going to make it today. But somehow the beauty of this extraordinary walk has revived me.

I am amazed by my husband's reactions to the dragon's back. He is revived and energised by its beauty and its flora and fauna. He has sometimes painted with watercolours, often painting from a photograph of some beautiful place we have visited. Last year, with a torn Achilles tendon and unable to play golf, he went on a painting course near our home. It was a two-day intensive course in Bradford-on-Avon with a local artist, and he came back with several large painted copies of favourite photos taken on other walks we have done. A few large frames from IKEA and they are ready to hang. He presented one to our daughter and son-in-law when they moved into their new home, a large three-floored Edwardian semi near Oxford. It remains propped against the wall inside the downstairs cloakroom, waiting time to hang things properly.

There is a family tradition of decorating the walls of the downstairs loo with a random assortment of hangings – old photos, certificates, quotes, documents. It's all slightly tongue-in-cheek and one that was regarded as being perversely odd and only somewhat amusing by our American friends when we lived in Virginia. To display one's achievements such as a degree, or a letter from Buckingham Palace, or even the family portraits from various years, in the 'restroom' and not on the walls of one's office was obviously one of the strange things that we Brits do. Kim and I each possess a framed copy of the prayers we gave when opening the US Senate in prayer – individually we've both had the privilege of being a duty Chaplain there for a day. These now also hang – alongside all those other special things – in the downstairs cloakroom, of course.

We pause on the ridge along one point of the dragon's back, slip off our packs and indulge in the mid-morning treat of hot coffee and a few squares of chocolate, to re-fuel. Butterflies sit poised beside us; distant farmhouses have closed shutters and undulating roofs. The sun is at last appearing, hazy but warm, and there is a gentle breeze. Life feels good, the walk feels good, *we* feel good. And ahead is the tail of the dragon, sloping down towards the road.

Singing in Mud and Rain

Slipping down towards the road. The mud is treacherous on the last downward part, thick and churned by wide cycle tyres. We stagger and slide, and are glad to get to the road, but it's only a couple of kilometres before we have to contend with mud and puddles and slippery farm tracks, going up and over and down three times as we cross three valleys. It's tough and tiring.

I try to sing a well-known old song, about fixing your eyes on Jesus when your road is rough and steep; Kim's song is more prosaic, about wallowing in the hollow in some glorious mud. The Hippoptamus Song makes us both laugh. He's always loved the Flanders and Swan songs. Childhood memories for both of us; my father built himself a record player and collected LP records, both classical and humorous, and he, too, loved the Flanders and Swan repertoire. He was always making things, whether a dolls' house for my sister and then one for my daughter, a toy garage for me and then another for my son; or developing his own black-and-white photos in the workshop he had created. As a young man he wrote journals during his travels, which were usually cycle tours on the continent with his friends; those books are in a box under my bed and I have yet to read them, mostly because his writing is illegible to me. Forced to change from his left to his right hand at primary school, his handwriting never improved; difficulty with writing caused him to teach himself to type with two fingers and he would hammer out letters and sermons standing at the tall wooden filing cabinet with the typewriter on top, as it hurt his back to sit for too long. He enjoyed walking, as long as he had the dog with him, but I don't recall him ever walking for more than half an hour at a time, the patient black Labrador at his side.

Thinking and talking of childhood songs and my father and trying to recall the words, we miss a turning.

Kim consults the iPhone again.

'We should be over there,' he says, pointing across the field to our left, which slopes gently uphill. 'We'll have to cross this field as I can't see any other way to get back to where we are meant to be.'

The field in question is a wheat field and the wheat is waist high. There are deep valleys of tractor tyres making deep pathways in between the wheat, and we walk in them, hoping there is no farmer with a shotgun watching us.

Seen on Facebook Yesterday

We are all just walking
Up the mountain and
We can sing as we climb
Or we can complain
About our sore feet.
Whichever we choose
We still gotta do the hike.

I decided
A long time ago
Singing made a lot
More sense

A Small Gift

Motivated by the thought of the next village, we keep going, hoping to find something for lunch. There was nothing near last night's accommodation and we have assumed we'll find something en route today. We gain the road and march along, but then I have to squat, and there is no cover again anywhere, just a long open road lined with long open fields. Not a tree or a bush in sight. I've given up caring. Fortunately no cars come along at that point.

We reach the small village of Salles-sur-L'Hers ten minutes before everything shuts for a long siesta. The little bio grocery shop is empty of customers and we chat to Michel and his wife. They have bananas and pears – fruit! And cashew nuts – protein! And organic chocolate – energy! We buy enough for tomorrow as well. As Kim is paying, Michel asks him about what we are doing, and is, as most people are, in awe of our plan to cross France on foot.

'Where is the local bar, please?' Kim asks Michel. He wants a beer today, not ice cream.

'Alas, it's no longer – it is *fermé*, closed, forever,' Michel says.

'That's so sad, no beer today, then!' Kim manages in French.

'*Attendez!* Wait!' Michel scurries outside, to return with an ice-cold bottle of beer. '*Un petit cadeau pour votre pérégrination* – a little gift for your pilgrimage,' he says, offering it with a beaming smile. Once again we are touched by the kindness of strangers who bless these foreigners crazily walking through their land. And interested that he calls it a pilgrimage.

We sit in the deserted village square surrounded by cream-coloured houses, the peeling paint of old closed shutters painted 'shabby chic' but actually original pale blues and sage greens; there are pots of bright geraniums dotted around, and more plane trees with their stippled bark. Lunch slips down nicely; we snooze for a few moments of siesta before setting off again.

Kim is cheerful. Is it the beer, or the fact that it isn't too far to the night's accommodation, which is situated on the road we are walking? The sign soon appears by the roadside, and as the rain has begun, we are greatly relieved to be nearing tonight's destination. What the sign didn't say was that the driveway is steep and over a mile long. I put up my umbrella, and we try singing in the rain. Rounding what appears to be the last bend, we are greeted by the sound of barking, and two small black-and-tan dogs leap out at us. We exchange wary glances but the sweet little creatures are very friendly and respond to pats and wag their tails at us.

A pair of tall stone gates are topped with seated gilded stone lions. There's a bit more driveway and the grand old chateau comes into sight at last. Nineteenth century, with a round tower at one end topped with a dark pointed slate roof, *Château Bel Aspect* offers BnB, so we tramp up to the grand front door, dripping wet, muddy of boot, looking, I suspect, exceedingly disreputable. The door is open; we are greeted by Madame Muriel wielding the vacuum cleaner. Everyone immediately tries to explain their appearance, with great laughs – us with our muddy wet clothes, she with her duster and vacuum cleaner. Unfazed by our state or by our 2pm arrival, she welcomes us in, plies us with tea and glasses of refreshing cold water, explains how she and her husband came from the Ardèche six years ago, bought the *château* and have been renovating it ever since.

'Was it your dream?' I ask.

'*Jamais*! Never, never, never,' she replies, shaking her head of dark long hair. 'I never thought we'd own a *château* and do bed and breakfast! It was my husband who dreamed of all this,' and she waves a tired hand around the large salon. 'He's always dreamed of living in a *château* and being his own boss.'

Living the Dream

My dream was to run a Christian retreat house, a place where those in Christian ministry in particular could come for rest and refreshment; where they could be spoilt and pampered, allowed time to *be*. Dreams, I know now, are hard work. We began the retreat ministry in good heart and anticipation, aided by a part-time housekeeper, and overseen and supported by a small group of Trustees. It was an enormous sadness that we couldn't sustain it long term.

There were five good years of offering retreats, of watching God work miracles in people's lives on a 'Re:Fresh Re:New Re:treat' as our tag line said. And for that we will always be grateful. But underneath, the price we had to pay, emotionally, physically, spiritually, maritally, was too high to continue. And so the decision was sadly made to sell the house and we hoped someone would buy it who might continue the retreat ministry. But that didn't happen and it has become a family home.

The Vine at Mays Farm was my dream; I lived it for a few years. I saw people arrive grey-faced, tired, worn out; and leave a few days later revived and with a spring in their step and a light in their eyes. It's time for me to be grateful for all of the good and to move on and embrace this new life. I'm glad we did it, even for a comparatively short time but I'm learning that life is a pilgrimage, a Grand Walk, and when it doesn't work out as I had planned, there are still good things to come and to enjoy. And that I'm stronger and more resilient from having lived through the tough stuff. I'm still upright and breathing and I am very grateful for that. And learning to see the beauty in the challenge.

We are led up a vast stone circular staircase and into a rather lovely bedroom. It is semi-circular, because it's in the tower, decorated in a rich flock wallpaper of green and pink and white, with a secret door in one little rounded tower wall leading to a newly installed gleaming bathroom. There are heaps of white towels, generous-sized bottles of lotions and potions, and, back in the bedroom, a huge double bed with crisp white sheets, piles of pillows *and no foot board*! There are two comfy armchairs, and a beautiful delicate desk with bookshelves stuffed with interesting French and English books.

Kim has a quick shower, washes out his clothes and rigs up our washing line in the large stone-floored cupboard. He then promptly falls asleep. I settle down to read, to write my journal, to relax.

Outside the torrential rain slashes at the trees surrounding the chateau. We won't be using the swimming pool. And it will be muddy again tomorrow.

> KIM:
> Having booked 2 duds in the last 2 nights I'm now back in favour with this chateau for tonight!

A Very Civilised Evening and More Dreams

Aperitifs are served in the drawing room at 7pm – chilled rosé, olives, tiny cheese squares. Hosts and guests sit and chat, and the conversation is slower or quicker, depending upon who is talking to whom. The other guests are a young couple. Josh is nearly thirty and left university after only a year to concentrate on other entrepreneurial ventures; Clarisse is French but moved to the UK when she was eleven and is totally fluent in London-speak. They are to celebrate his thirtieth birthday at the chateau later in the year and have come to finalise arrangements to bring twenty-four friends for a weekend in deepest France. As Josh is now an events organiser, it should all be fairly straightforward, but this is a big occasion and he wants it to be exactly as he wants it to be. Plus, they are going to look at a large property tomorrow with a view to it becoming their base, so with Kim's love of property and entrepreneurial adventure, he and Josh have a lot in common.

In London, Josh and Clarisse can't really afford to buy a flat; but here in the Midi, for slightly less than €500,000, they can buy a fifteen-roomed chateau with two *gîtes* and nine hectares of land. He plans to run events, to have a couple live rent-free in one *gîte* to provide all the labour needed, and he will commute to London occasionally when necessary. It sounds idyllic, I think, and wish I were thirty years younger. What a dream! But then I catch a glimpse of Muriel looking so tired; and her husband, who has appeared in time for aperitifs, has been strimming all afternoon in the grounds, and is so thin that he seems all skin and bones. It's hard work running a large old chateau like this.

An hour later, Muriel realises she ought to serve dinner – there's fresh green salad, huge baskets of different breads, dried duck, a piquant dressing. Then *cassoulet*, the regional speciality, with lots of beans, followed by apple tart.

'There's a reason the word "pulse" is found in "repulsive",' Kim says, whispering his usual joke to me; he detests beans and their relatives.

KIM:
The *cassoulet* was interesting – quite a lot of beans and I had to eat *cassoulet* once as it is very much the dish of the region; but I've done *cassoulet* now, thank you.

We retire early, and are lulled to sleep by the song of the rain.

* * * *

'Shall we stay another night?' Kim says sleepily next morning. 'It's pouring with rain, this bed is so comfortable and tonight's bed is just a mobile home on a camp site.'

'Get thee behind me . . .' I say, forcing myself out of bed.

Chapter Five
Finding a Song in the Rain

I'm raring to go, full of beans after *cassoulet*, a deep, deep sleep, and lots of lovely protein for breakfast. Plus Miles Moreland, the hero and instigator of my French walk, has emailed me back about the Walk. We stand on the chateau doorstep for a photo in the rain and Muriel is most amused by my raised umbrella. The track continues on from the stone gates and up what is meant to be a path but is now a small river. Kim trails behind me as I splash cheerfully up the stream.

'Your get-up-and-go had got up and gone yesterday,' he says, 'but it's back with a vengeance today!'

The two kilometres on this track are perhaps some of the most difficult and toughest so far. Although we say that every time the going gets tough. This is thick, squelchy, beige mud that clings heavily to our boots and weighs us down, so the little road at the top is a welcome sight. Today we are grateful to Mr MacAdam, who invented tarmac; we make the decision to stay on the little back roads. The fields are flooded, the ditches full, the roads disappearing under thick, slimy, pale mud. And it was Welsh Mr Hooley who invented the road surface in any case.

Encouraging Words

Even steep hills feel very easy to me today. The difference is almost unbelievable. Poor Kim is struggling. I tell him that for someone who has had a stroke, shingles and a torn Achilles all within the past eighteen months, he is doing incredibly well and I am impressed he has got this far.

'Encourage one another and build one another up.' (1 Thessalonians 5:11 NIV)

How would the world differ from the one we know if we all encouraged one another instead of pulling each other to pieces? One of the things we noticed when we first began visiting the States regularly in the 1990s was the difference in media interviews of politicians. In England we were used to journalists and interviewers doing their cynical best to undermine and 'cut to size' those whom they were interviewing; and that becoming normal down through the levels of society.

In the USA, by contrast, we heard mothers praising their children, friends telling one another how good they looked or how well they were doing, strangers commenting on something about you that they liked or appreciated. Even members of the congregation thanking their vicar for a helpful sermon, rather than 'your jacket clashes with the church carpet', which I received on one occasion in London after preaching my heart out.

The difference between the two countries in this respect is no longer so apparent, as the USA culture has become more critical over the intervening years. But it made me stop and ponder whether I, too, was guilty of criticising more and encouraging less, when it could so easily be the other way around were I to retrain my mind and my words. *'If you can't say anything nice, don't say anything at all,'* I told my children. I wish I had applied it to myself more, as well, and made a difference to others.

Encouraging when the going is tough makes a surprising difference, we discover as we plod along a hard surface yet again.

The next valley is pretty, a vibrant pale green of little undulations with a row of stately trees along the top of the ridge to our left. We cross the regional boundary to the sound of the cuckoo. It's one of the sounds we hear a lot as we walk. I'm conscious of birds singing and chirruping all the time; occasionally squirrels or magpies chatter at us; and cars are few and far between although today a few pass us swishing and swooshing in the rain. There are farms with cows behind bars in the farmyard, languorously switching their tails and sometimes mooing at us. Today, we've passed from the vineyards of the Minervois and the Aude regions, to the breadbasket of the Haute Garonne, with its wide fields sweeping up and down the hills, and the occasional field of cows. Still lots of ducks everywhere, and now big fields of geese who honk and flutter. We are literally singing in the rain – huge laughs, soggy feet, cheerful tunes to keep us going.

Camping in the Rain

After a mere ten wet, muddy miles, we stagger into Calmont, the town on the L'Hers River where we are to spend the night. It's 1pm; the store closed at 12.30pm. We head on to the *boulangerie*; that closed at 1pm, just moments before we reached its doors, having paused at the store. We hurry on to the café/restaurant. It's closed all day on Mondays. This is France; what did we expect? Kim checks his iPhone for alternatives and discovers that the mobile home campsite where we are to stay the night has a restaurant on site and that, according to the website, it's open now. As we have to be self-catering in the mobile home, that's good news. The bad news is that it's over the river and a little way out of town. But there's nothing else to be done, we don't want to sit out in the rain and wait for the shops to reopen later, and so we decide to carry on and utilise whatever the campsite has to offer. It's clearly signposted with bright painted boards showing tents and little mobile homes surrounded with animals and children and kites. It looks promisingly charming.

And is totally deserted. We walk around the main buildings, all of which are firmly closed, restaurant included. Looking through the windows we are not too sure we would want to go in, actually. The toilet block is unlocked though, and moderately clean. Very useful. There is a large herb garden, overflowing with delicious rosemary and lavender, and sheltering some grubby tables and chairs. Sitting down, grateful that the rain has almost ceased, we share out the remains of yesterday's fruit and nuts and chocolate. The man who lives in an adjacent house appears and tells us that *la propriétaire* arrives at 2pm each afternoon. Sure enough, she does arrive just after 2pm, a small bustling woman with olive skin and the thickest south-west accent we have heard so far. She leads us on a guided tour of the toilets and showers and my heart sinks.

'Is there no toilet in the little house?' I ask. She is surprised that we are not camping and tells us that, normally, walkers camp, and that's fine even when it's out of season like now. Nothing is open yet for the summer as it's still June and the French families don't holiday until early July.

'I think I did book a mobile home and we don't have a tent,' Kim says, and she takes us to a 'single unit' as she calls it. There are a few of these little 'units' or tiny mobile homes spread around, with low hedges in between each one; the units were once painted white or grey or pale blue but now are mostly very dingy. There are vast puddles everywhere, the outside camping furniture is stacked up beside each one, and the curtains are pulled across each window, making the entire place look totally abandoned. *La propriétaire* unlocks the door of one of the smaller, closer ones, and proudly ushers us in.

It looks like the interior of a small caravan from the 1960s, retaining what I am convinced are its original soft furnishings. To my left, a small kitchen area runs the short width of the living area and comprises a steel sink, a few open shelves with basic utensils, and a calor gas ring and oven. Straight ahead, one door leads into a tiny 'bathroom' with toilet, hand basin and shower, none of which looks fit for human use; the other door leads into the bedroom with a tiny 'double' bed and thin mattress, but no sheets or blankets. In the living area to my right, a small table with a bench either side, its uprights with long cushions covered in much-used thin yellow-and-red patterned fabric. At least, I think it was once yellow and red. It's hard to tell now. It's damp and everything looks slightly stained and very forlorn.

La propriétaire is chatting away in the thick accent of the *sud-oust*, although it's difficult to make out what she is saying.

'*Lentement, s'il vous plaît*, slowly please,' we plead.

Eventually we are able to make her understand that yes, we did book and yes, it is for just one night, but no, we haven't brought our own sheets and towels. She bustles off and returns with sheets and pillow cases and I am relieved to discover they are crisp and white and clean. After she has left we realise she didn't bring towels. But by that stage she has left the site. We never do get any towels and I have to admit we make that an excuse not to use the disgusting shower while we are there. It's only us and the cabin smelt fairly bad before we ever sat down. We decide we will wear the same clothes tomorrow; there's no point in washing anything as it won't dry in this damp atmosphere. And we do each carry a quick-drying hand towel made of a special water-absorbing fabric, which will be fine for a quick rinse-off.

We have no matches so we are unable to light the gas ring, but there is a drip coffee machine and I use it to make a cup of tea – at least we have Lapsang teabags and we both drink it black. Grateful for small mercies, we are revived by hot tea.

KIM:
The trait of the English is to make the best of a bad job. The weather has been the worst so far and this is the grottiest accommodation so far and we have laughed more today than probably any day of the trip so far.

A Shopping Trip

By 3 o'clock the rain has completely stopped and we don flip-flops to sooth our tired feet and wander back to the shops. It feels extraordinarily strange to be walking in flat shoes with nothing on our backs. Almost liberating, yet also missing something. Kim enthusiastically decides to go to *la boucherie* counter in the tiny supermarket and buy steak and cook up a feast. While he deliberates at the butcher counter, I find a frozen lasagne readymade meal, a box of matches, a bottle of red wine and a ready-bagged and washed salad. Sorted. And eggs and coffee for breakfast.

Everything is packed into a cardboard box (we should have bought a backpack after all – will we ever learn?) and as we set out again the heavens open and we are now slipping around in our flip-flops with a rapidly disintegrating cardboard box. We are soon in floods of giggles at the whole situation and that's before we've even opened the wine. We hurry back to drown our sorrows with a rather nice bottle of Corbières. And the good news that a little church attended by a friend, in upstate New York, has decided to donate two hundred and fifty dollars to each of our chosen charities. We are overwhelmed and grateful again for friends and for people's generosity.

Lights out soon after 9.30pm. I fear I won't sleep in the damp little unit. The next thing I know it's breakfast time.

* * * *

'What time will you be leaving tomorrow?' *la propriétaire* had asked us.

I shrugged. '*Peut-être*, perhaps eight-thirty, maybe eight,' I replied.

'Oh no, not that late,' Kim says, overruling me. 'We need to leave by seven, or even latest seven-thirty, to have a good early start.'

We wake at 7.30am amazed that we have even slept at all, let alone for so long. There's the treat of scrambled eggs and freshly made hot coffee for breakfast, before setting off in cool watery sunshine. And more freshly made coffee to fill the flasks. We've made the decision to stay down on the plain, on the roads, as the footpaths along the ridge will be thick mud after so much rain, and so we walk quickly for a couple of hours, the snow-capped

Pyrenees to our left. There is definitely more snow on the highest peaks. We make good time, in spite of stopping for photos, for ibruprofen for his shin and my hip flexor, for passing cars. French drivers don't slow for walkers and Kim's arm suffers a stone thrown up by a fast car.

'Ow!' he cries as the sharp little stone flicks into his arm. The car driver is oblivious and speeds off into the distance. I investigate his arm but fortunately there is no wound except his pride. 'This makes me more aware of how I have been as a driver myself,' he acknowledges as yet another car whizzes past us on this tiny back road. There are no pavements, of course, and sometimes not even a grass verge on which to step out of the way of passing traffic. But we still prefer to be here rather than coping with the thick mud on the foot paths; it clogs up on our boots into heavy lumps and clods, slowing us down and making the walking exceedingly uncomfortable and difficult. Maybe we are mad to attempt the road, but it is meant to be a back road, not a highway. There isn't a lot of traffic, it's just that what there is seems to be trying to break the speed record.

The Ariège and L'Hers rivers are full and fast, muddy waters carrying boughs and twigs and rubbish along at an appallingly fast rate. Tiny green young sunflower and maize plants stand in water. Some sloping fields have had landslides and the mud has swept the plants away. It must be devastating for the farmers.

Discovering Almond Croissants

The little village of Cintegabelle has two wonderful places: a bookshop and a bar. The former is sadly closed today so the alternative is coffee, Kim's first choice anyway. We sit outside, under the awning, for strong coffees; Kim longs for a croissant.

'Just there, round the corner,' says our middle-aged waitress, who wears tight jeans and a sparkly striped top. 'Go further up the street to the *boulangerie*.' As always, we are surprised and grateful that it's fine to eat the produce from one place while drinking coffee at another.

The *boulangerie* is artisanal and Kim returns with warm croissants oozing a delicious thick almond filling, and topped with icing sugar and toasted almonds; we demolish them and he returns for two more. They are the best we have ever eaten, of course, and we enjoy a second coffee with them, just as the rain begins again.

'*Zut alors!* It's June!' despairs our waitress. 'And we have had so much rain!'

The maps are checked again to ensure the best possible route in these conditions, but we still don't want to take the main road, and so opt for the shorter route along a small back road but which still involves a couple of miles on footpaths. Just as we reach the beginning of a long grassed track, the heavens really do open and empty out some of the heaviest rain either of us has seen. Kim says it reminds him of the rains in Singapore when he and his family lived there many years ago. Sheets of heavy rain, obliterating the landscape, cascading down the banks, pouring from the trees, soaking us through – or is it sweat from being so hot and sticky when walking wrapped tightly in waterproofs? Rain bounces in big puddles. We pause under a vast chestnut tree, hoping for some shelter for a moment of respite, watching the rain bouncing in the large puddles forming across the path.

'It's no good,' I say, 'it's not going to stop raining any time soon – look at those black clouds coming our way.'

I realise that my feet are swimming. The rain is seeping in over the top of my boots, presumably. It is a struggle to get to Autorive; the rain pours down our faces, drips off our noses, falls off the long grass on to our boots. In fact, this is miserable. Whatever made us think we wanted to walk across France? My dream of pottering along in the warm French sun, stopping at little village markets for smelly cheese and fragrant tomatoes and fresh peaches for our picnics recedes, and I stumble along longing for this wet nightmare to come to an end.

Eventually the town sign appears.

Wet, Wet, Wet

'Photo opportunity,' Kim says and I stand by the sign and hold out my arms demonstrating how much water is running off them. But now there is a spring in our soggy steps.

'It can't be far to lunch, can it?' I ask.

'What do you fancy?' Kim sits in the bus shelter to look up recommended restaurants for lunch on his phone. '*Crêpes?*'

'Ooh yes,' I say. 'We've not had *crêpes* this trip yet. Is it far?'

I should have guessed that on this rainy day, the suburbs are long and strung out; it seems ages until we reach the old town, the bridge and then the *crêperie*. It's on a little side street, and there's a charming terrace with wicker chairs and tables under a striped awning, wisteria climbing frantically up the walls, a doorway to the interior, passing the kitchen where the young male chef is busily creating *crêpes* and *galettes*. On a sunny day, the outside area would have been charming for a pleasant lunch.

We drip inside; a bucket is produced for my umbrella and it is kindly suggested we might leave our backpacks to drip by the door before we are shown upstairs to the dining area. White paper covers each dark wood table; the walls disappear under dark French prints; the windows are steamy and the sound of chatter and laughter fills the air. There are several large groups as well as singles and couples, and there is a general air of *bonhomie* in the room. I have failed to point out that the rest of me is just as dripping as my umbrella and backpack, and as we sit I notice a puddle forming under my arm on the paper tablecloth. Sitting still when damp leads to a chill; I am soon feeling decidedly cold and shivery.

'Why don't you change?' Kim suggests.

'Into what?' I retort, and he reminds me I have all my clothes with me in the backpack. What a relief to find dry warm clothes and do a quick change in the cloakroom. Strangely it has also a shower and a washing machine. Both are extremely tempting.

Four courses for €14 each, including a *pichet* of wine. It would be rude not to. Blue cheese salad, a honey and four cheese *galette*; vanilla ice cream and *crêpes* with a salted caramel sauce; coffee. I am now wearing a dry shirt and a cashmere sweater; we are warm and dry and feeling so much better. But it doesn't last long, for we have to don damp jackets and backpacks. I discover that my jacket has dried on the inside though. It is indeed waterproof, and is doing its best in the circumstances.

Another Little Gift

Later, much later, after the rain eases and we are showered and rested and settled into the basic studio accommodation that was converted from a garage, there is an expedition back to the town centre, to potter in the shops and enjoy a modicum of normality. The old buildings remind us of north Norfolk: flint and red brick in horizontal stripes. One wall of the studio has retained the flint too. The air is still damp but the rain has ceased, for a while at least.

In the *biologique delicatessen et épicerie*, Kim is persuaded to do a little *dégustation* of a delicious Muscat. It's a local Muscat, an ancient grape varietal grown by the Romans in this area, and actually smells and tastes of grapes in a way most other wines don't. One wine connoisseur describes it as an eerie wine because of that, but I like its crisp, dry freshness and would happily have tasted more!

'One chilled bottle, *s'il vous plaît*,' Kim says, wanting to buy me a treat, but alas there is no other chilled bottle available, and we have nowhere to chill a bottle in the studio. He settles for a bottle of beer to take back for the evening, and explains in more detail to the assistants what we are madly doing.

'*Alors, un petit cadeau pour vous, Madame!*' and I am presented with the opened bottle of chilled Muscat to take with me. I don't complain.

Setting out

Canal du Midi

Kim gets lost

Carcassonne – a damp arrival

Up to the
Dragon's back

Singing in
the rain

Picking
our way

De boue!

After the chateau

Chocolate box village

Celebrating halfway

More than a little damp

Rural idyll

Picture perfect

Final leg

We made it!

Chapter Six
Finding Out How to Keep Going

'I wanted to go home at 3am,' confesses Kim. He has had yet another terrible night, with back pains, shin pains, foot pains. Neither of us has slept well as the bed was not particularly comfortable and there was an outside light shining in the window with only a thin muslin curtain to diffuse it. He rubs 'Icy Hot' pain relieving cream strategically in various places, and happens to glance down at our boots, which we propped against the radiator, hoping they might dry out overnight.

'There are holes in your boots!' he exclaims. 'They really have worn right through on the heels. No wonder you had such wet feet yesterday. It wasn't going over the top; it was seeping in from below. What do we do? Should we get you some new ones?'

I am reluctant – new ones would not be worn in and would cause blisters, I am sure. And where do I find new ones? Might these just last the trip – it can't rain like this for another two and half weeks, can it? We load up and set off – in heavy rain, in boots that have not dried out overnight and which are leaking.

First stop is the *boulangerie* for coffee and croissants; another customer is telling the girl behind the counter about a local house which has collapsed in a landslide.

'We've never known rain like this,' she tells us. 'It's a disaster.'

Maybe it's the dampness causing the pain in Kim's front left shin. Or maybe it's the constant pounding on hard surfaces. We pause again to take ibuprofen before striding off along flat little roads. Where there are hills to climb, we notice that they are much easier to do – we scarcely alter our pace, taking them in our stride, and simply keeping going. This walking must be doing something for our fitness levels, after all. The rain begins again, an incessant thundering on my umbrella. It drips off the sides, bounces on the pathway, dampens trousers that then stick to the legs. Too late for donning waterproof overtrousers; we are already wet.

As there were no self-catering facilities of any kind in the studio, we are looking for more hot coffee by mid-morning, and the map shows an *épicierie* in Miremont. Cheered by the thought of at least a bar of chocolate and hopefully coffee, we speed along, but a detour into the centre of the village reveals only an old shop long since out of business. There is an internet facility, and a place for collecting mail-order parcels, and a primary school. But, yet again, no bar or *pâtisserie* or *boulangerie*. Even rural France is losing the traditional individual shops, and catering instead for our modern online world of shopping. We've noticed this in several villages, and it feels rather sad.

On the other hand, I haven't seen a single one of those old-fashioned French public toilets where you had to spread your feet wide and squat over a large square porcelain edifice with a central hole. There are some benefits in modernisation for which I am profoundly grateful although there have been several occasions already on this trip when even one of the old squatting cubicles would have been much appreciated.

Maybe I should relinquish my much-loved coffee.

The Rigours of Pilgrimage

The only coffee we have now is from yesterday, still in the flask, and cold.

'Think of it as iced coffee, to refresh you,' I say, cheerfully emptying in one of the little packets of sugar I rescue from saucers to store away. Even the sugar doesn't disguise how disgusting the coffee is. However, the clouds are lifting and we remove our jackets and enjoy the rolling pretty countryside now emerging from the low cloud as the sun begins to burn it off. There are still a few wheat fields, no vineyards whatsoever, and lots more maize. Every so often as we crest an incline, the Pyrenees might come into view, on our left as always, and they continually lift our spirits. There's something about hills and mountains.

'I will lift up mine eyes unto the hills; from whence cometh my help come. My help cometh from the Lord, which made heaven and earth.' (Psalm 121:1-2 KJV)

Both of us learnt those words in earlier days, Kim at boarding school singing in the school chapel, and I at my father's church singing in the choir. We recite the comforting and exhilarating words – encouraging one another in the words of Scripture to keep going, to keep our eyes on the Lord, no matter what.

'We could go home, you know,' I suggest.

'Except that we have house-sitters, who have nowhere else to go,' replies Kim. 'It's just first-world problems.'

I know this; and am encouraged by friends on social media.

'Ah, the rigours of pilgrimage!' writes one friend.

'C'mon, you can do this! Keep going and when you've had enough, just keep going,' enthuses another.

'I'm exhausted just following your progress!' writes someone I don't even know, who seems to be following our social media threads.

We have to keep going. Rain or no rain. We are not giving up. Not yet.

'Keep us strong, keep us going, Lord,' we pray.

The houses are no longer built of stone; red brick is becoming more normal and as we walk into Saint-Sulpice-sur-Lèze the old buildings are a mixture of brick and timber. Two enormous juggernauts blast past us and the backrush causes me to stagger rather alarmingly. There is an old bridge over the Lèze River, and then we are into the town square and surrounded by the old, slightly faded grandeur of half-timbered buildings, faded shutters, arched colonnades, and a couple of shops.

We are just in time to order the lunch *formule* €5 at the *boulangerie*: *Croque Monsieur* (warm), chocolate tart and Orangina for Kim; warm *tarte au chèvre et poireaux* (goat's cheese and pear tart), a *café éclair* (I have to have some caffeine injected somehow) and an ice-cold water for me – all for €5 each. We sit at a bright lime-green metal table in the arched colonnade. There are cobbles underfoot, amazing old brick archways above our heads, tubs of red geraniums lining the edge of the colonnades, hollyhocks tall against brick walls. It's the beauty of France for which I've been longing and I'm blessed by it. *Thank you, Lord*, I think.

It's one of the prettiest towns we have yet seen and we love it enough to walk around after lunch and explore the little streets. Normally we are loath to add extra miles, but today it is worth it and we meander in the afternoon sun, enjoying being touristy, and aware that we have only a very few kilometres to go before we reach our next rest stop: thirty-six hours to recuperate!

Time for a Rest

L'Abre is an old brick farmhouse lying on a small plateau below the long rolling ridges of the Volvestre. The path follows the ridge, bordered by thick white flowers and grasses, and the views on both sides are stunning: to the left beyond the house, wooded hillsides; to the right the plain with a small town surrounded by fields and low hills. We race along, longing to reach our place of rest, and are stopped by the sound of beautiful little bells. There is a flock of rather lovely sheep in the field beside us and they are wearing small golden bells around their woolly necks. They follow our steps, keeping pace with us as we reach the end of the track.

Rounding the corner and we are at the farmhouse, to be greeted by the bath. It's an ancient, long, narrow, copper affair, with a once-white interior, languishing in the shade of the trees.

'A BATH!' I exclaim. 'I've been wanting a bath for nearly two weeks! I'm almost tempted to use it later!'

The front of the house – or maybe it's the back, we never do discover which is officially the front – is covered with pretty creepers. There is an old brick terrace along its length, widening by the door to be covered by a pergola with wisteria providing shade. There are terracotta pots and tubs, in various stages of disintegration. Old chairs of wood, metal and plastic are strategically placed under shrubs or by tubs, inviting you to rest a while. The grass is not worthy of being called a lawn; it stretches gently down to a wooden fence separating the garden from the swimming pool, and draws the eyes across the valley to the hills in the distance.

Further along there is a large *potager*, a rich, verdant vegetable area of tomatoes and lettuces and beans and peas and herbs.

A Red Admiral butterfly suns itself on the fragrant jasmine. In the afternoon sun L'Abre looks enchanting, shabby chic and welcoming. There is a large circular iron table in front of us, gaily covered with a green-and-white-check cloth, and a tray laden with tea, coffee, beer and wine. Helping themselves are three men, their boots and jackets spread out over the chairs to dry in the sun. They greet us affably and we soon discover that they are good friends who walk a week together each year. This year they are walking from Toulouse on the Santiago de Compostela route, and they had had our hostess collect them at the top of the track in her car! We feel very virtuous having walked all the way down the long path.

Clémence hears us and comes running out. She is warm and friendly, obviously slightly scatter-brained, thin and wiry with a comfortable old long denim skirt and a blue-and-red-check shirt. She informs us all that this morning she took the previous walkers back up the track in her car, and then adds they were Dutch, walking from Holland to Santiago, a journey of nearly six months. We now feel rather amateurish.

Clémence says our room isn't quite ready yet, but she will make us fresh tea and we can sit in the sun and relax. And would we like to use her washing machine and hang our clothes out to dry on her washing line at the bottom of the garden? I think we smell. And probably look very unkempt. But it's a very kind offer and one I gratefully accept. It will be a treat to have everything properly washed and dried in the sun tomorrow. I am suddenly overwhelmingly grateful for what at home I completely take for granted –the ability to wash and have clean clothes. And amazed yet again at the kindness of strangers and the enormous welcome they extend to weary travellers.

Nothing to Do but Eat

At the far end of the house is a vast room of three walls built with stone and brick; the fourth side is completely open to the elements, overlooking the garden and out towards the hills. The ground slopes down gently to this end of the old farmhouse, so there are steps up to the kitchen and private family area, and at the bottom of the steps is a large stove. Across the room is an enormous butcher's block with blue painted legs and sides, and here Clémence and Hugo cook dinner. It's all very informal and very friendly. The five of us who are guests are invited to be seated at the long table, at right angles to the butcher's block, and Hugo opens bottles of his own unlabelled wine and pours generously into an assortment of coloured wine glasses. Hugo is a wonderful chef: cheerful and generous with a great heart.

We eat pâté on toast, then a delicious courgette terrine with a carrot and cabbage salad; duck shepherd's pie, something I make at home with those enormous tins of duck confit one brings back from French holidays, but this one is very delicious, and is accompanied by a tossed green salad. Then a chocolate-and-pear dessert appears. And as we eat, the conversation ranges far and wide, in a mixture of French and English and nods and gestures. Hugo has a wicked sense of humour and teases me when I decline more of his wine. The crisp white is followed by a chilled fruity red; too much and I won't sleep tonight. They bring coffee but I ask for a *tisane* – and Clémence takes me to the herb garden in her *potager* to choose my herb. I opt for lemon balm and she picks it and pops it into a china teapot.

I think I could live here. Although I would want to have a spring clean first: I think the original cobwebs are still in position. Hugo

121

brings out the photos of the seventeenth-century farmhouse when they bought it thirty years ago, and of all the renovation work and rebuilding they had to do. It looked pristine when it was finished; I am not convinced anything has been moved or dusted since.

Our fellow travellers are leaving in the morning and ask for a lift back up the track. We learn a new word: *trichee*, cheat; *nous n'avons pas trichee*! We haven't cheated – yet.

Kim and I both sleep for ten hours. The old wood shutters have kept out the early morning sun, the two single beds are comfortable and far better than one small double for tall people like us, and we feel rested and ready to do absolutely nothing.

Breakfast is in the small conservatory on the other side of the house – front? back? – overlooking a tiny strip of grass, a low hedge and then their own small vineyard. The room has a variety of old carpets and rugs covering the floor; there is a large sideboard holding a dusty assortment of clocks, pictures, trays, china ornaments and various *objets d'art*. Pots of tall, green, stripy house plants. A tall bookcase is stacked with cobwebs and books upright and sideways. An old wooden ladder leads up to a loft. And in the centre of the room, an oval table with a faded red-velvet cloth reaching the ground. On it is the most delicious breakfast – freshly squeezed orange juice, lots of excellent coffee, and an amazing whole hot fresh brioche, sprinkled with tiny lumps of sugar.

We linger, knowing we have nowhere to go and nothing to do. Clémence, meanwhile, is bustling around and asks me for my dirty washing. Even I can smell that it stinks and I am most embarrassed, but she bravely bears it away to the machine. The sun is trying to come out; we head for the pool with our Kindles and journals and Clémence comes with sun loungers and cushions and towels, which we offer to help with but she tells us it's fine and it's our rest day and we must rest!

Soon she is sweeping leaves from the old red tiles on the terrace; running a farmhouse even without a farm is a full-time job – they have the house, the pool, the *potager*, one pasture and the tiny vineyard. She does bed and breakfast and Hugo works in town during the day. I'm finding it difficult to sit still and do nothing, especially while she is working so hard; I need a more engrossing book on the Kindle to be lost in for the day.

Journeys

Perhaps I should start with my daily Bible reading. I've not been very good at keeping in touch with the Lord over the past days. The daily Bible study notes I normally read were going through the New Testament book of Romans and it felt as though I had missed so much and now it was coming to the tail end and I couldn't manage to catch up. So I gave up. But today it's the Old Testament book of Exodus, chapter 12, preparing for a journey on the brink of a new life. It feels most appropriate as I read about the people of Israel being ready to start an adventure with God, eating the Passover meal standing up and fully dressed.

This is walking into the future with God; no dressing gown and slippers – this is a long-term journey, walking in a manner that is constantly ready for whatever new thing God may call us to, ready to follow him wherever he leads us. It was a Day To Remember: leaving yet remembering later with an annual celebration. It feels so appropriate to me, to us: making a complete break with the past, its heartaches and failures and traumas, and going forward in a new way with the Lord.

And I think of the prayer written by Susannah Wesley, mother of Charles and John, who not once but twice endured the total loss of her home by fire:

Help me, O Lord,
To make a true use of all
disappointments and calamities in this life
in such a way that they may unite
my heart more closely with Thine.

Can I truly pray that too?

It's wonderfully peaceful sitting by the pool. Little lizards flit past at our feet; the sun shines again, although it's not warm enough to swim. Once, this homestead might have been my ideal but I'm more realistic in my old age. Old houses take a lot of upkeep and guests coming and going can be an arduous way to earn an income. We learned that the hard way, as one of our grandsons would say.

Taking on an early-sixteenth-century Grade II listed farmhouse in need of total renovation, and then offering it as a retreat house to burnt-out clergy in particular (although 'normal' people were welcome too), was both a huge privilege and an enormous stress in every way. I would welcome guests with their pale-grey faces, red-rimmed eyes, drooping shoulders. Take them breakfast in bed, cook them fresh meals, offer prayer times in chapel, listen to their stories and pray with and for them. And a few days later, after rest, long walks or long naps, they would bounce away with a spring in their step and colour in their faces. We made a wildflower garden, grew tomatoes and herbs and lettuces and beets in the Polytunnel, picked apples and pears and damsons and raspberries in the orchard, lit log fires in the winter. Getta, our lovely Romanian housekeeper, came in most mornings and did the housework and the laundry and grew more vegetables; I did the bookings and the advertising and the press releases to try to encourage more people to come. Those who came loved it and many came more than once; but there were never enough guests to raise enough income to pay the huge bills and maintain the house and satisfy the Conservation Officer's demands. And when we eventually realised we would sadly have to sell, it took over a year of buyers pulling out and of the Conservation Officer's demands.

I am sure the stress was partly what caused Kim's stroke and ocular shingles. It definitely enlarged the difficulties in our marriage as we danced our 'do-si-do' around each other, not talking of how we were feeling, not admitting to being stressed or unhappy or not coping, pretending that everything was all right. Believing that God would provide all that we needed. Maybe we didn't need to be doing the retreat house.

A year ago we did finally move and now it's time to put it all behind us, to remember that we have a future ahead of us, to find ourselves in France. I think it was C.S. Lewis who wrote something about while you cannot change the past, you can start again from here and live the future well.

We are walking into our future.

KIM:
This place is the definition of rustic – rusty chairs which sink into the ground after the rain; cobwebs everywhere, long grass, faded cushions. But Clémence could not be kinder. She calls us to lunch in the middle of our lazy day and produces the most delicious feast: a plate of cheeses, her own home-made pressed ham, more of the courgette terrine. An absolute feast. All washed down with half a litre of Hugo's red wine. And coffee with homemade hot chocolate muffins. We tell her she is a wonderful *cuisinier*, chef; she laughs and says, *non, non*, Hugo is the *cuisinier;* she is a *chef pâtissier*, and she made the brioche we had at breakfast.

A Little Cheating

Dinner is just us and our hosts, and we chat and laugh a lot. Once again it is a gourmet feast in the big open-ended room, with Hugo cooking *aiguillettes de canard* – duck fillets which come from underneath the *magret* – in a stroganoff sauce made with Juraçon wine.

And then Clémence surpasses herself with *baba au rhum*, freshly-made rum babas, served with her thick cream and decorated with pretty blue borage flowers.

If you indulge you bulge, I write on social media, accompanying a lovely photo of the pretty concoction.

Bulge on, it's worth it, replies a friend.

I walk to eat and eat to walk, I remind myself. But tomorrow morning – please may we cheat? Might we avail ourselves of a lift along the nine-hundred-metre driveway and across to the other side of the main road as we have to cross it on a bend and it looked busy and dangerous.

'*Bien sûr*, of course,' Clémence says with a smile. '*Bonne nuit!*'

Chapter Seven
Finding the Halfway Point

Clémence hugs me tightly and hands me a white paper bag after breakfast. It's one of her homemade brioches to take with us. We've already devoured most of the one on the breakfast table, freshly warm from the oven, and now here is another one for later. It's becoming a new favourite!

She and Hugo have been so kind and generous to us; we feel we have become friends and she and I decide to connect on Instagram so that she can follow our Grand Walk and I can see her lovely creations.

'We will come back,' we promise. 'And you must come to Bath!'

She takes us in her ancient Peugeot up the long drive, across the frighteningly busy main road and a little way up the small road opposite, depositing us on to the next stage: week three.

Trichee? Mais non, non! Being safe and realistic!

We walk over the hills and down to Noé, passing the Garonne River which has burst its banks and is a small, angry, thick tsunami. Coming into the little town, Kim pops his head into the estate agent's door as we pass.

'Is there an ATM here in Noé?' he asks.

'*Oui*, just up the road at the *supermarché*, it's only two kilometres.'

But two kilometres there and two back is too far a detour to add to today's journey so we carry on to the next little town. The track we are on is long and straight and flat; there isn't much to see and it's actually a trifle boring. But it's easy walking and we stride along, glad to be walking on again.

There is an ATM inside the *Bureau de Poste* in the next small town, but randomly the Post Office is only open from 2–5pm on weekday afternoons. We thought that was when everything in France is closed for a long leisurely lunch? We drown our sorrows in hot coffee served in disposable cups from the *boulangerie* and as we sit on the benches in the very modern town square-cum-carpark, a man approaches us.

'*Vous faites une randonnée?*' he enquires. 'Are you doing a long walk? I saw you earlier and passed you in my car. I, too, walk long distances and I wondered where you are heading? Are you on route to Compostela?' He sits and chats with us for a while in Franglais, as we explain what we are doing, and then he wishes us '*Bonne continuation!*'

We have been made to feel welcomed and encouraged. Yet again, we are glad of the way people here treat strangers, welcoming them without fear or prejudice. *OK, Lord,* I think, *I am beginning to get the idea. Less of the cold British standoffishness I often wear, particularly towards those I don't know or of whom I feel perhaps a little scared. Or even those I just don't seem to like very much. Help me to see Jesus in those I meet. Help me to extend your kindness and welcome to all. No matter how they are dressed or what they look like or the colour of their skin.*

Local Church Spires and More Rain

Today's theme is churches and their spires. In this part of France they are mostly brick with pointy spires, and can be seen peering over treetops from some distance away. Kim decides today's project is to photograph them, to relieve the monotony of the walk. The villages are not particularly noteworthy, the little road is monotonous and the countryside is flat, viewless, lost in mist. I am somewhat cheered by a lovely Pyrenean Mountain dog coming towards us, lumbering along behind his owner, its shaggy black-and-tan coat damp. I pat and stroke him, marvelling to Kim at the dog's size.

The thin dark-skinned man harrumphs at me. I think it's meant to be a greeting.

As I stand up again, reluctantly bidding the dog farewell, the rain suddenly begins in torrential earnest. I reach for my umbrella, and we turn to find shelter under a nearby full-leaved tree in order to remove our backpacks and find their waterproof covers and our jackets.

'Not again!' Kim groans. 'This is unbelievable in mid-June!' It is indeed June 15th, and we are very nearly halfway across France.

My feet are hurting a little from all the hard-road walking of previous days; and my left toes are beginning to complain, in spite of the protective toe caps I'm wearing, the padded walking socks, and the old boots which are well worn in and have never ever caused blisters before. At lunch we perch on a convenient bench and I remove boot, damp sock and toe caps and enjoy an hour of freedom and fresh air circulating between the toes.

We eat pizza slices, Clémence's delicious brioche and then I find two peaches in a side pocket which I had totally forgotten were there. They are beyond ripe and have squished messily into the brown paper bag. We are not fussy and devour them greedily with the juices dripping everywhere. It's still damp; we are sitting in a modern village, with passing foot and vehicle traffic on three sides. Do we care? No we don't. We are just grateful for a seat, some food, and a rest! And there is an ATM on the outside of the *Bureau de Poste*. Our feet dry a little – in avoiding the roads today we have been on smooth, slick tracks but the long grass we had to traverse at one point was wet and both my boots are definitely holey underneath the heels.

On we trudge, enduring the damp and the mist and now on a small back road again. Gradually the sun breaks through, waterproofs can be removed, and raindrops on hedges and verges delicately twinkle in the sunlight. A few wild roses lift their heads again. Breezes pulse with the scents of wild rosemary and thyme. The birds wheel and call; we wish we knew their names but we can still enjoy their antics and song. And from far away across the fields, another cuckoo. It's now pleasant and warm and suddenly things feel much better.

I'm always amazed at how much better I feel when I am warm and dry! This Great Walk is marvellous, I think. I'm thoroughly enjoying myself.

For now.

A Luxurious Event

Up a small gradient, which a few weeks ago would have felt and looked like a steep hill, and we are into another small village, Pucharramet, where we will spend the night. There's an enormous pale-red-brick old church on our right, a primary school on our left – and the children are watching a funny puppet play in the school yard, and there is much laughter and noise. We smile and wave and they laugh at us too. Turning left in the centre of the village, ahead of us is a long, high, red-brick wall, with a pair of tall Confederate-blue ironwork gates. Kim pushes open the right-hand one and we find ourselves in an Italian-style garden – gravel paths run between the parterres, there are vast terracotta pots with palms, bamboos, fig trees. Roses and herbs fill the beds; rosemary with tiny blue-grey flowers, lavender in full purple, the bright green of marjoram. A large single-storey house ahead of us is three sides of the square, built of red brick and flint, nestling inside the walled garden; outside the right-hand wing of the house, elegant wooden chairs are arranged under large cream parasols around little tables which are loaded with trays of coffee and cups and biscotti. Two men and a woman are relaxing and chatting but leap up to greet us.

'Welcome, welcome! You must be Kim!' A stately but very charming man in his late sixties greets us. Tall, erect, and dressed like an English gentleman with his blue-and-white striped shirt, faded tan shorts and dark blue slip-on loafers. His English is beautifully correct with that enchanting slight French undertone.

Be still, my beating heart.

'Take off your packs – leave them there!' He beams a welcome. 'Come and sit down with us!'

He ushers us to seats with the others, and introduces us to his sweet Moroccan wife and to their friend who has called in for a short visit as he is on a cycle tour of the area today. Monsieur plies us with tea, coffee, fresh madeleines. Kim leans back and crosses his legs and relaxes. He has brought us safely to the next place and it is looking good thus far. As usual, there are enquiries about our Walk, relaxed conversations, plenty of time to sit and chat. More

131

tea and cake is pressed on us, the sun begins to get lower, it's an enchanting late afternoon, but now I am longing to shower and change into clean clothes.

Eventually, Monsieur takes us up the low steps and in through the big double front doors in the centre of the building. They lead into a polished red-tiled hall stretching from front to back of the house, lined with chairs and books shelves and a grandfather clock. There's an old dark wood hat stand, sporting panamas and berets and boaters. The door immediately to the right goes to the billiard room, filled in the middle with the green-baize table and on the far wall by a well-stocked bar, complete with loaded glass shelves, and large French posters on the walls. The door to the left leads into a formal sitting room, piled high with glorious books on nearly every surface – small tables, a sideboard, a small armoire. Monsieur explains that the sitting room and bar are 'common' areas; beyond the bar is their private wing and beyond the sitting room is the visitors' wing. We are the only visitors tonight, and we have been given a lovely bedroom; but for me the best part is the large adjoining Art Deco style green-tiled bathroom with its enormous green bath raised on a dais and reached by two long steps. It is magnificent.

A BATH.

A whole bath – and a separate shower unit.

The first thing I do, after dumping my pack unceremoniously on the floor in the bedroom, is turn on the bath taps full blast and tip in most of a jar of bath salts. The hot water rushes and steams and looks very inviting.

As I undress and turn, I catch sight of the back of my right shoulder and upper arm in the long mirror on the wall above the two hand basins. I thought my shoulder had felt a little uncomfortable during the past couple of days but I hadn't really paid much attention or had a large enough mirror to see more than my face. Now I am horrified by a large area of extremely sunburnt, peeling, flaking skin. And memories of Day 4 flit across my mind, lying down on the grass after lunch, the sun behind my head and on the top of my shoulders while I was wearing the new sleeveless shirt. In spite of all the creams and oils I massage in every day, I have bad sunburn. I had thought it was just the straps of the backpack rubbing a little. As ever, I ignore pain or actually don't feel it. 'No sense, no feeling,' my parents always joked about me, and it's true. I have a high pain threshold unless and until I am at the dentist when I feel even the slightest twinge. But the rest of me is resilient and strong. The sunburn looks rather scary; the skin is peeling off in large circles.

I sink into the warm bath and soak and soak. Bliss for aching muscles and peeling skin.

A University Wine Degree

Kim, meanwhile, is chatting with Monsieur, learning that he is a retired Professor of Oenology from Toulouse University – is it only France that would have professors to lecture about wine? The two men discuss one of their favourite topics and soon there is an invitation for us to join our host at the bar for some wine tasting before we head out to dinner.

So at 6.30pm, we join *M. le Professeur* in the billiard/bar room. He stands behind the highly polished bar, and produces a bottle of Jurançon. We have only ever tasted the sweet white Jurançon wine, delicious with pâté or dessert; this is dry – Jurançon sec – with hidden depths. Kim swirls and sips and pronounces it stunning. He and the *professeur* discuss wine and rugby and wine again.

'My wife and I have lived here for over thirty years,' he tells us. 'It is a seventeenth-century house; our children grew up here. But now, we are – how do you say – empty nesters?' He laughs. 'Once I had retired from the university, I decided to begin a new business of bed and breakfast.' He waves a hand around with a flourish. 'I often have groups who come for some gourmet food, with wine pairings and tastings.'

'Who does the cooking?' I am intrigued.

'I love cooking too,' he confesses. 'It is relaxing for me. So I have taken cookery courses, studied food, experimented. Now I enjoy very much to cook for my guests when there is a large party here.'

Riverdance

'Is there such a dinner with wine tasting tonight?' We are hopeful. Sadly, because the beautiful handwritten framed menu on the hall wall looks very appetising, there isn't one offered tonight as we are the only guests. Instead, we head to the only place in the village offering food this evening, where Kim has now phoned to book a table – La Maison de Terre community restaurant.

'The website said something about there being live music tonight,' he says, as we head through the narrow streets.

The community centre is staffed by two friendly young people.

''Allo! *Entrez*, come in!' says the bright young woman, her frizzy hair caught up with a bright scarf tied in a jaunty bow on top. Her denim dungarees are baggy and cover a spotty shirt. It's all very like the *'Allo 'Allo!* programme on TV years ago and I have to stifle my giggles. The small café, the 1940s hairstyle, the bright-red lips and wonderful greeting. It's France during the war.

Her companion is a tall, thin, dark man whose English is just as good.

'Der eez only one plate this evening,' he says.

'No menu?' says Kim rather sadly.

'No, but it ees ver' good. It ees tapas and wine. Pleez, you sit where you like. We bring you plates and wine.'

Kim's French is now remarkably well-practised, and he is soon chatting and laughing and explaining to the young woman that we are walking across France and that he is very hungry.

'I'll bring two plates for you,' she promises him. The 'plates' turn out to be generous portions of delicious cheeses, dried meats, olives, roasted vegetables, nuts, olive oils and dips, served with enormous hunks of fresh warm bread and a full bottle of dark red wine. It's all locally produced – and there are bottles and jars available to buy on the tall dresser by our table.

We are the first to arrive and begin; but soon the long, low room which opens out of the entrance bar is filled with other people too – families, couples, young and old. The village turns out for this Friday evening once-a-month event. They all know one another and there is a great deal of chatter and friendship; small children run around, the baker arrives with people's evening bread orders, and soon the place is heaving.

At 8.30pm tables are pushed into the middle of the room, and the musicians move into place around them. They have arrived carrying their instruments, eaten their tapas and are ready to make music. Anyone in the village can bring any instrument they like, and they make music together once a month. It is absolutely amazing. Three accordions, a dozen violins, a cello, two banjos, a couple of violas, a trumpet, music stands and sheets of music all appear. This month it is Gaelic dance music – and suddenly it's Riverdance and everyone is tapping their feet and having a great time.

It is an extraordinary evening, full of togetherness and community. People are alight with enjoyment, contented, enjoying family time and we feel just a small part of it. Children run and dance, babies sleep through it all and the elderly nod off around the edges of the room.

But we are tired after our day's exertions and we leave them to it and head off to a comfortable bed. We fall asleep immediately and sleep soundly for eight hours, the music still lilting in our heads.

* * * *

Day 15 already – and today we will reach the halfway mark. It feels momentous. Can we truly have walked so far already? I feel a little giddy with excited anticipation. Halfway!

We are aiming for the halfway village by noon, and hope to find somewhere to sit and celebrate. But first, *M. le Professeur* serves us breakfast in his private kitchen. He is frying eggs and bacon!

'Only for the English,' he says without the glimmer of a smile. 'Not for anyone else. I know you like your cooked breakfasts.'

It feels like a real treat. He fills our flasks and we are ready for what may lie ahead.

It's a mere 59F as we leave the village and my jacket is on. I don't like wearing it unless it is absolutely necessary; it's a lightweight waterproof and windproof bright-blue affair and is great at its job but I feel restricted when wearing it under a backpack and it can become quite damp inside with sweat when there's exertion on a hill. But it's cool this morning and I'm glad of the extra layer.

After we've been walking for ninety minutes a village comes into view and, yet again, the thought of hot coffee and fresh pastries is very tempting. Is it worth a detour to see if such things exist? Grateful for modern technology, we discover on Google maps that there is the promise of both a shop and a café, so we trek up the road and are rewarded with delicious coffee and then *l'épicierie* to buy provisions for lunch.

An Unexpected Silence

The day is dank and grey; as we cross the fields on wet and muddy paths, the rain begins again and my feet are soon damp. Walking through a thick forest adds to the heavy atmosphere but it is at least on a wide and easy path. As we go deeper into the lush green woods, the path widens, the rain stops and hazy sun filters through the leaves. There is a faint hint of mist and fairyland magic. There is no-one else around and when we pause for me to find a tissue, there is total silence. We realise how much noise we make walking – the waterproofs rustle, my walking pole clinks on gravels and stones, Kim's pole, lodged in his pack, chinks on his flask, rain drops patter.

Stand still and we hear the birds singing, the leaves shivering, the drip of rain from the trees. God's creation, the beauty of nature, feeds our souls. I'm reminded of Genesis and the story of the Lord God walking in the garden. He must have enjoyed the glory of its trees and flowers and colour. Or is that too English a garden? *'Walk with us, Lord, we welcome your Presence with us.'*

Suddenly, flies and midges begin to hover around us, and there is the unmistakeable buzz of mosquitoes. Bring back the rain! We hunt for insect repellent and spray our faces and necks and then stride on quickly, now longing to be out of the woods. The easy track makes for fast walking and we make good time on this long pathway. The overhanging trees form a tunnel and eventually we spy cars passing the end of it and realise we are nearly there – nearly halfway. At the junction with the road, leaving the forest, we turn right up the little road, and see the signpost to Forgues.

'Nearly there! Nearly halfway!' I say, and it feels exciting. Even if we get no further, we will have made it halfway across France – but actually that makes us even more determined to walk the whole way.

Halfway Across France

The road to Forgues takes us up a steep tree-lined hill at the top of which, on the right-hand side, is the village sign.

FORGUES.

We are halfway across France!

I laugh and cry and laugh again. It is very exciting and quite an achievement! Kim is also excited. He kisses me and then kisses me again. We cling to each other and I'm glad and grateful for this man all over again. *'Help me to forgive and to forget, Lord.'*

'Well done us!' he says, and we pause at the village sign for photos, selfies, thinking that will be our 'halfway' shot. Rounding the corner on to the main village street, we are greeted by bright red, white and blue bunting zig-zagging across the road. 'They've put out the bunting to greet us,' Kim says and he is optimistic of a great welcome. It's 11.30am and we are halfway across France! The excitement is obviously contagious because on our right is the village community centre and it's buzzing with activity. A white marquee hosts long tables covered in bright-pink tablecloths; chairs are being set out and the tables decorated with jam jars of wild flowers. A few small old-fashioned tractors are being manoeuvred into position nearby; music blares out from the loudspeaker. There are park benches around the open gravelled area, and we are intending to perch on one to rest, but as we approach it, a small plump woman detaches herself from the preparations.

'*Vous êtes d'où?* Where are you from?' she says, coming to greet us with a warm welcome. 'Today, it is our village fete and there will be a feast later this afternoon. Would you like to stay and join us? It would be a pleasure to have you!'

Yet another wonderful welcome and show of hospitality, to two travel-weary if enthusiastic total strangers who happen to have wandered into the annual village fete.

So we tell her of our Walk and enthuse about our halfway point now in Forgues, and she is thrilled that it's this particular village for our celebration! She leads us to the beer stall where there is a choice of beer or beer to toast our success. For the first time in my life, I have a whole beer. It comes in a plastic cup but tastes far better than I feared it might.

Entertaining the Strangers

People gather round as our hostess conveys the news of our achievement. They congratulate us; they tell us we can use the toilets in the hall and to have some *frites* from the big trailer, already cooking up a feast. Beer and chips: why not? Someone takes a photo of us on Kim's iPhone, and he uses his technology skills to write 'halfway' across it and post it on social media. We are having a great time; this is fun and we are blessed to have received yet another wonderful welcome from local people who have no idea who we are or where we have appeared from, yet extend warmth and bless us with hospitality. And again I am reminded how often I am fearful of the unknown, of the person who looks 'different' to me, of putting a cool barrier between me and those I don't know.

'Do not neglect to show hospitality to strangers, for by doing that some have entertained angels without knowing it.' (Hebrews 13:2)

When have I done that? What does it say to me about the vast migration of people at this point in history? All those refugees who risk their lives in fleeing from their country in the hope of finding freedom and fulfilment in a strange land far from home, tossing around in tiny boats on rough seas, walking hundreds of miles with only what they can carry, living rough even in cold northern winters. I am chastened by the welcomes we have been given on so many occasions, the small but significant gifts we have received, the gestures of help and support.

And I think, *this is a lesson I do not want to forget,* and wonder how I can implement such a welcome to others I encounter – the homeless, the unwanted, the underprivileged, the foreigner.

* * * *

The Second Half Begins

Taking a deep breath, shouldering our packs once more, we bid farewell to the lovely villagers of Forgues, and plunge into the second half of this momentous Walk. At least the rain has ceased. Coming down the road out of Forgues, there is a garden centre on our right, with a large open area of trees and shrubs planted in straight rows. It is completely under water, a large expanse of brown, thick sludge, and the ditches on either side of us are running with more.

'We still have fourteen kilometres to go,' Kim tells me, and we try to stride quickly along the long winding road. A steep incline brings us up to views again, this time of long vistas of gently undulating rolling fields of slowly ripening wheat, interspersed with low dark hedges. The roadsides are long grass verges with everlasting wild sweet peas bursting into pinks and purples and reminding me of home. Low grey skies feel oppressive but we are passing from the flat plains of the Garonne and the Ariège, and coming into the Gers, where the regional speciality is foie gras.

We perch on a rickety bench for lunch – I am convinced it is actually in someone's garden, as French houses often don't have hedges and fences to mark out privacy; but Kim needs to sit down and rest his aching shins. My feet are uncomfortable too – the hard surface certainly takes its toll. I undo the laces and remove boots and socks; and inspect my boots. I discover that not only are the soles peeling under the heels, but that the upper is coming away from the sides on my right boot. No wonder my feet are wet and uncomfortable. These sturdy trusty boots have walked a long way on several pilgrimages, daily walks at home, and now halfway across France. They have finally had it. Now what do I do? They have to go back on for now, and I cram damp, slightly sore feet back into the sad boots.

Weary, and no longer with the buzz of the halfway mark, we decide to go the shorter routes for the rest of the day, choosing the road rather than the longer, wetter, muddier footpaths. It's a busy road, however, and the enormous lorries are hurtling alarmingly at us as we walk along facing the oncoming traffic. Eventually I cross the road and walk on the right, with the traffic coming from behind. At least I can't see what's coming at me and it feels less scary. Kim and I both hold out our walking poles in our left hands so that the traffic has to pull out to pass us. It seems to work; coming towards us, the lorries and cars ignore us and hurtle straight at us; coming from behind, they are forced to slow and pull out. It feels a lot safer.

I am plodding along, my eyes on the ground. I am feeling tired, my feet are damp and uncomfortable and I am longing to get to our night's accommodation, when I suddenly look up to glimpse beauty. The sky ahead is dark charcoal; outlined against it on top of the hill is a glorious French *manoir*, an old manor house illuminated by the sun from behind us to a brilliant creamy-white against the sky, the green fields sloping away in front of it. A living impressionist painting. It's worth looking up and not being downward trod. *There's a sermon illustration in that*, I think to myself.

Many of the roads leading to small towns and villages are lined with tall, straight poplar trees on either side, informing us we are nearly there, and Samatan is no exception. The trees lead to an old grey-stone bridge topped on both sides with troughs filled with scarlet geraniums, white petunias, cascades of dark blue aubretia. And right by the bridge, the first building in the town, is the Logis where we are to stay – it's not the far side of town! The relief is palpable. Although it's an old building, the inside is very modern French décor, and the bedroom has large white decorations in weird and wonderful configurations on the grey walls, silver lampshades, purple and black bed linens. We don't care what it looks like; there is so much to love. A kettle, so we can make a decent cup of tea to revive us; an enormous semi-circular fully tiled shower with plenty of space to trample out clothes; a heated towel rail on which to dry them. But even more than that – a large brown box from Amazon, addressed to me, is waiting on the table. Curiosity demands that I tear it open at once. My dear husband has ordered a gift for me: a new, replica pair of walking boots! I am overwhelmed and nearly in tears with gratitude. Yet again we have reason to be grateful for modern technology. I gratefully hug him, emotional tears in my eyes.

Washed, changed, rested and somewhat revived, we head down to the restaurant. Samatan is the centre of the foie gras region, so dinner is an extravaganza. We take precautionary antacids before bed and are asleep well before 10pm. It has been a long day of battling roads, wet feet, emotional celebrations and nearly seventeen miles.

'I'm not setting an alarm,' Kim says. 'I think we both need to sleep as long as possible.'

It feels very indulgent.

Binning the Boots

The next morning we wake slowly, neither of us wanting to get up and get on; neither of us wanting to walk another step. It feels lovely to lie in a comfortable bed, snoozing. So it's a huge effort to haul ourselves out of bed and make coffee and pack up yet again. I try on the new boots. They seem a good fit, but should I carry the old ones in case of discomfort or even blisters? These are identical and the old ones have never given a moment of pain until this walk; but they are surprisingly heavy to carry. I throw them in the bin with great relief, and we stagger stiffly over the town bridge in search of breakfast and provisions.

Even though it's Sunday, there is already a bustle and hubbub; not, alas, a market – that's on Mondays here so yet again we've missed it. Today, it's the big boules championship, held on the car park of the enormous building proclaiming itself to be the *'volaille et gras marché'* – the indoor foie gras and goose market. There are teams of men playing boules and covering the vast expanse; most players are dressed in blue or grey, a few wear traditional berets.

There is a very small, mostly male audience; the cigarette smoke creates a thin smog.

Around the corner is the *boulangerie* and already there is a small queue. Here are the women, buying *tartes* and *gâteaux* for Sunday lunch, exchanging greetings with one another and with the shop assistants. There are rows and rows of beautiful *pâtissières* – chocolate and coffee and fruit and cream – all lined up in serried ranks, tempting and calorific and hardly sustaining.

'*Pas de quiches ou pizza?*' we enquire, wanting to buy something for lunch. No quiche or pizza? But no, not on Sundays apparently; only sweet things. We settle for *pain aux raisins* (for me) and *pain au chocolat* (for Kim) and adjourn to the bar to consume our breakfast with more strong coffee.

The day is composed of several long, steady climbs – only of about three hundred metres, but by the time you have done that six or seven times in a morning carrying twenty pounds on your back, you are longing for the flat Gironde again. There are no cars on the little roads today and we stagger along, until Kim realises we have missed a turning. We stop to check the online maps, grateful again for the internet, and he chooses an alternative route – and discovers it's half a kilometre shorter than the original route.

Every little helps.

The tiny hill-top village of Saint-Soulan has very few houses, a huge stone war memorial obelisk, a tiny old church, and a marvellous picnic table and bench with a view looking back the way we have come – miles and miles of rolling hillsides and fields as far as the eye can see.

It also, to our huge amazement, has a tiny stone-built public 'WC' with a lift-up-the-latch pretty blue door, surrounded by fragrant lavender bushes. It turns out to be immaculate and real

– no hole in the ground affair. And with plenty of soft white toilet paper. Small things give enormous pleasure and make us grateful for what at home we take for granted.

Lacking a Welcome

Then it's back to the ups and downs; along the ridge tops there are majestic views on all sides – across the immense countryside with fields of ripening crops, dark clumps of trees, and in the far distance once again, the Pyrenees. One more really steep climb will bring us to our midday rest point. Today's lunch stop is at Boulaur. The twelfth-century *Abbaye de Boulaur* can be seen across the valley for several miles, a warm limestone building nestling in the hillside, a pointed tower at one end. Climbing up the steep road to the village makes us puff today – we really are tired after a long day yesterday. The signpost to the *abbaye* also mentions *peintures murales* from the fourteenth century. I love old frescoes, and quicken my steps.

The road to the *abbaye* turns off to the right in the centre of the village, past glorious old stone and timber houses with hollyhocks and roses and blue-flowered rosemary brightening the pervasively grey day. The whole area feels deserted – shutters are closed, there's no-one around, no sounds. We turn in at the wide-open abbey gates, and see spacious trim lawns, old stone buildings of church and monastery, wide gravel paths. A small collection of once-white plastic chairs nestles under a spreading tree on the far lawn and looks ideal for a picnic rest, but first I want to see inside the old abbey. It dates from 1142, was restored in 1949 and now houses Cistercian nuns.

Peeking around the old oak door into the ancient church I am surrounded with heaven. Of course – it's Sunday! The white-robed nuns are singing *a capella* – two lines of nuns stand in the choir pews facing one another, their black wimples disappearing into the haze of incense. One comes out into the centre of the chancel and pulls a long bell rope three times; the nuns turn in choreographed unison to face east, and silence descends as the bell rope is pulled again three times. There is a good-sized congregation standing, too, and they bow slowly, and then there is stillness for a few moments. The nuns turn back again to face the congregation and bow, before filing out by a side door that perhaps leads into their main quarters.

The congregation turns to leave by the door where we are loitering, mesmerised. We stand back to allow people to pass us, as we wait to go and be tourists in the church; no-one speaks or acknowledges us – we are just two curious backpackers after all.

We gawp and gasp at beautiful faded frescoes of angels and Bible characters, at carved heads and painted ceilings, before retreating to the chairs under the trees. The congregation must have repaired inside for coffee for they begin to emerge again in ones and twos from the main building as we sit munching yesterday's baguette, and ripe peaches and frangipane croissants bought this morning. Again, no-one acknowledges us or even smiles at us. It feels slightly odd, especially after the usual warm welcomes we have received elsewhere. Do we look exceedingly strange or frightening? Do we smell? (Yes, probably, but not that bad, surely?)

The only friendly presence is a small terrier, white with turned-down pale-apricot ears and matching spots. He is timid and needs some persuasion to allow himself to be petted, but begrudges us every mouthful. He sits with us for some time, watching people come and go, watching us devour our lunch.

They look curiously at us but no-one approaches us. There is a slight feeling of being overlooked, and of the church being the one place where we have not been made to feel welcome. It's rather sad. I would have appreciated a loo, but feel unable to go and ask someone. We pack up, take our rubbish with us and bid the little terrier farewell. He trots off inside the door. He obviously has no fear of being unwelcome. Maybe he belongs.

'Is that how visitors to our churches have felt?' I say, thinking back to past parishes and churches. 'Unwelcomed, with no smiles or even acknowledgment of their existence? No wonder people don't come to church unless they have to for a funeral or the occasional wedding.' It seems very sad and makes me think of times I must have ignored visitors or not been as friendly as I might have been. I vow to do better in the future. It is another salutary lesson.

A Room with No View

Tonight we reach a traditional *chambres d'hôtes* – an old-fashioned French BnB. It lies at the end of a long driveway sitting on top of a small ridge and lined with cherry trees. At the end of the driveway is an L-shaped farmhouse on the right, while on the left a low fence surrounds the small outdoor swimming pool. Monsieur comes limping to greet us; weather-beaten of face and round of body, he greets us enthusiastically, and leads us on the stony track around the left-hand edge of the house to the adjoining outbuildings at the back, which are now transformed into simple guest rooms. There is a tiny 'double' bed, a couple of chairs, and a large carved mirror-fronted wardrobe. He opens this triumphantly to show us a small mini bar, a kettle, English teabags and fresh milk.

'Dinner at eight,' he says. We exchange glances. That's hours away yet!

'Please, please, Monsieur, could it be earlier?' Kim asks. '*Peut-être*, perhaps at seven?' A compromise of 7.30pm is agreed. The French evening dinner hour is always so late for those who have walked all day and not eaten much at lunch time.

'Hope you have a lovely place in which to stay tonight! xx' texts a dear friend.

'It's interesting,' I text back. 'Basic: loo has a curtain rather than a door, the bed is tiny, and there's no window in our room, just a stable-type door. But there are pluses to be grateful for, such as a kettle and tea bags; and crisp white sheets. xx'

She replies, 'I love your thankful spirit; crisp white sheets can of course make up for a lot! xx'

I hope she's right.

European Relationships

I brew a reviving cup of tea and take it outside to drink whilst sitting on the green plastic chairs in front of our stable door. But even at 4pm it is too cool to sit outside for long, and I soon retreat inside again. So I am a little dismayed to see supper laid for us on an outside table on the terrace at the front of the house, under the shade of the vine that staggers across an old wooden trellis overhead. But it is slightly warmer by the side of the main house, sheltered in its angles, and sitting there is delightful. Monsieur brings us a peach kir as an aperitif, followed by a very duck-y but surprisingly delicious supper – sweet ripe melon with his own home-cured dried duck and thinly sliced *Pyreneën* mountain ham; roasted *magret* of duck (from the farm up the road) with his wife's home-grown vegetables and homemade ratatouille; and local cheese served with cherries from the driveway trees. All served on lovely, antique blue-and-white china plates, and washed down with generous quantities of the local red wine. A veritable feast, proudly served by our host and greatly enjoyed by us.

We retire to bed and sleep comes quickly. Until at 11pm there is an incredible noise. Monsieur has warned us that there are guests from Spain staying in the room next to ours, men who have come for the good hunting available in this area, and they tend to return late at night – and he harrumphed in displeasure. Sure enough, they are late and loud and inebriated and clatter around until after 1pm.

KIM:

'They were *un peu bruyant*, a little noisy,' I tell Monsieur at breakfast, and he agrees, and says that the Spanish are always like that and he doesn't like having them but they come every year and are always noisy and late. No love lost between the European countries again, then.

A Snail Village

'I couldn't get comfortable last night. I was awake on and off, and really, really wanted to go home,' Kim admits to me before breakfast. He looks jaded and I offer a hug.

'You'll be fine after some coffee, I'm sure,' I enthuse, 'and we can go slowly. Don't worry – you'll be fine.' He looks reassured, but inwardly I am worried that today will be too much for him if he hasn't slept and is feeling under the weather. Hopefully I can encourage him along.

We are still tired and the tiny bed didn't help matters. By the time we have been entertained by Monsieur (we never did see his wife) over bread and jam and milky coffee, and packed up, and tied our laces, it is 9.30am before we leave. But today it doesn't matter – we know we can't arrive at tonight's house until after 4.30pm, and the sun is trying to come through the clouds.

Hearts lift as we take a short detour to look at Castelnau-Barbarens. It is what is known locally as *un village d'escargot* – a snail village. Concentric little circles of streets wind around and up the hillside, culminating in the church at the top. This is definitely the prettiest village we have visited so far, we tell each other! Built of beautiful pale-cream stone, the tiny houses and cottages have dark sloping tiled roofs, enchanting gardens and are linked by steep little alleys and flights of steps. One flight of faded brick has terracotta pots of bright-red geraniums on each step; jasmine and roses overhang old stone walls; poplar trees are scattered through the village. The old church has a separate bell tower a few feet away, with a circular stone staircase inside next to the old clock machinery. And next to the tower, a thoroughly modern public toilet, before we descend to the valley below.

As we begin the long, slow pull of the incline over the next ridge, I find my second breath and realise that I can do this. It's no longer such a huff and puff and I am a lot fitter than I have been for many years. I stride ahead in my new seven league boots and assume that Kim is not far behind. In fact, he has stopped to talk to a couple tending to a small row of vines.

'I assumed it was father and daughter,' he tells me, once he catches up again as I wait for him. 'Did you see them? A tall strapping man and what appeared from a distance to be a tiny little girl who seemed to be doing all the work of spraying the vines. Turns out she is the old lady, who has always had just enough vines to make her own wine, and that was her son helping her.'

We are in the land of grain – the breadbasket of France – and the old lady prefers her own wine so always has three or four rows of vines to keep her in wine for the year.

There Might be Dogs

Over the top, down the other side, and we leave the road and dive off down a farm track, going around a small lake. And then we come to a chain-link fence and a sign: PRIVATE. Up ahead, the farm track is visible, leading past the back of a house, and I am fearful of meeting huge ferocious guard dogs.

'It will be fine,' Kim assures me. 'The map shows a footpath, and the sign and the chain are for cars and other vehicles, and it's too far to retrace our steps and find another route.'

My fear combines with the mud, the incline and the straw beneath our feet, and I begin to panic and hyperventilate. He meanwhile is loving the off-piste adventure; tiredness gone, his long legs stride over the straw with ease and I find it hard to keep up.

I hate this. I don't want to walk another step. I want to go home. I can't breathe. My pack is heavy. I can't breathe. I want to go home.

'Have a sweet,' says Kim and stuffs a toffee in my mouth. I plough on and am greatly relieved to get past the house, leave the straw and get on to a rough path with comfy grassy banks on which to lay back and have a coffee stop and some chocolate squares to restore my equilibrium.

KIM:

We are sitting having coffee watching an enormous piece of farm machinery driving up and down a large field, mowing the hay. The birds of prey follow the tractor, wheeling above it. You would think they'd be scared of this great noisy beast, but they follow it, having learnt that the little animals which live in the field are being exposed and I've just watched a couple of the birds swoop down and pick up little rodents. Mice perhaps or voles or baby rabbits.

The Wood Shed

The drizzle begins again as we go over the next ridge, but we are still able to see and to sense the change of scenery. Kim surveys the scene in front of us.

'The wheat fields have given way to wood and forest and tree; we've come from the wine cellar through the breadbasket to the wood shed,' he says. He loves wood. 'The oak is used for making wine barrels but I'm sure it's also good for winter fires.'

Another up and over and this time the air changes for the better – it's dry and warm and the sun finally appears again. We are hoping for a decent lunch at (another) Auterive, as tonight's BnB has no food available anywhere nearby; so the plan is a full lunch and then nibbles later. The restaurant is indeed open, and the *menu de jour* is just €14 for five courses and includes a *pichet du vin*. It's warm enough to sit in the courtyard, and we sit for two hours and eat our way leisurely through the entire menu.

First the red round pot of soup is placed on the table, for us to help ourselves to the beef vermicelli broth. It's followed by little white succulent fillets of fish, served with tartare sauce and green salad. Much to Kim's dismay, the main course is chilli con carne (*boeuf de Gers*, we are informed, beef from the Gers region) so he eats very little of that as he dislikes both chilli and kidney bean. He makes up for it with dessert while I plump for cheese. And then coffee. It is a lovely respite and we are glad to sit and relax.

And as we do so, the sun strengthens, the temperature rises and by 3.00 pm we are happy to be walking in the shade of the trees which line the road. Tonight's BnB hostess has already told us that she is a nurse and will not be home from her shift until 5pm. We follow paths and roads, up hill and down dale, until a final really steep down and then steeply up again into the village. At the bottom of the steep down, there is a wide grassy area surrounding a square pond. Sitting beside it is a fisherman dressed in thick yellow oilskins; he is a permanent fixture to welcome you to the village. There are a couple of homes behind him, one surrounded by tall trees.

We're not sure where the house is but guess it must be at the top of the village, and struggle up the final steep incline, watching a mother and child run down the steep grassy bank in their garden beside the road – they have parked at the top and are coming down to their house at the bottom, behind the tall trees. We toil on up, turn right alongside the hedge, and find their car and the tiny gap in the hedge – which of course leads all the way back down to their house and the gate which was at the bottom by the fisherman: it's our BnB.

A French Family

Camille comes running to meet us; she is small and neat with very short dark hair. She looks very . . . French. Warm and friendly and welcoming, she draws us into her kitchen, making us tea, offering to do a load of laundry for me. Yet again we are overwhelmingly grateful to these lovely French people who are extremely hospitable and go way beyond what might be expected. Camille had told Kim when we booked that there was no restaurant in the area for our dinner and that we could use her kitchen to fend for ourselves. He has asked if she could get us some eggs so we could just make a quick omelette. Soon, Victor, her husband returns and the World Cup football interests of the men have them sitting drinking beer on the terrace overlooking the swimming pool while the children, a boy of twelve and a girl of six, cavort in the water to cool off.

'This is the first time this summer it has been warm enough to sit outside and to use the pool,' Camille says. 'We have had so much rain and it's been unusually cool for this time of year.'

Victor produces a bottle of wine; nibbles are laid out; he lights the outside grill and is soon cooking mushrooms and omelettes.

'You will eat with us?' they ask. 'Come and sit.' We all gather around the table on the side terrace. There is pâté and baguettes, then mushroom omelettes. They have kindly cooked what we asked for! Mathieu, the twelve-year-old, is learning English at school and he is encouraged to talk to us in English.

'Where do you live?' he asks. 'Have you visited London?' We congratulate him on his courage and his English but his little sister laughs at him. He scowls. He's nearly a teenager.

Later, as Camille hangs my washing all around her kitchen to dry overnight, she says, 'Please, help yourselves to breakfast tomorrow. There's bread and jam and coffee and tea. We all leave soon after seven.'

'What about the key and locking the house,' I ask her. But she says the door is never locked so just to let ourselves out – and no, there is no extra charge for dinner, laundry or breakfast. It's her contribution to our sponsored walk.

But the bed is a three-quarter size futon in the corner of the study. It is exceedingly uncomfortable, and it takes us ages to fall asleep, and we sleep fitfully, bumping into each other. It doesn't bode well for tomorrow.

Not Another Step

I wake, cross and grumpy. No, I don't want cake and bread for breakfast; no, I don't want to heave that heavy backpack on to my shoulders; and no, I don't want to walk another kill-o-metre. I want to go home and sleep long and deep in my own bed. After two consecutive nights in tiny uncomfortable beds, plus a night of noisy Spaniards, I'm tired. I'm longing for fresh fruit, yoghurt, protein.

'We've got this far, we're going to do it all,' Kim encourages me. 'Look, there are some small pots of yoghurt in the fridge – I'm sure Camille wouldn't mind you having one of those for breakfast.' It's his turn to cheer me; together we will do this Walk.

Even if it kills us.

On Pilgrimage

The sky is clear, the air warm, as we set off at 8am. It looks as though it might be the first day with no rain for ten days. We have a long haul up, some of which is really steep, but as ever the reward is the far-reaching view from the ridge top, of undulating fields and thick dark green forests and hills in the distance; there are poppies waving in the long grass of the verges. And then the long descent into L'Isle-de-Noé, where Camille has assured us we will be able to get a coffee mid-morning. We are both tired, both quiet, walking in silence but still in this together. I try not to groan too much, but every step is beginning to feel uncomfortable. And I really do feel very tired. I try to think of the mediaeval pilgrims struggling with this mud; bitten by mosquitoes without our modern relieving analgesics; with no bed other than a barn perhaps, or under a hedgerow; and with a little plain bread, probably stale, to sustain them. I am blessed.

There is an information sign about the Gers region by the beautiful old bridge, and a bronze statue of D'Artagnan, minister to Louis IV. His full name apparently was Charles de Batz de Castelmore d'Artagnan, and he died and was buried at Maastricht in 1673 while serving the King, Louis IV, with faith, courage and devotion. He is probably the most famous musketeer, even though he wasn't one of the Three and only becomes a musketeer at the end of Alexander Dumas' story.

The village is at the confluence of the Grande and Petite Baïse rivers, the large and the small, and was an important rest place on the pilgrimage route from Arles to Compostela, but the small hospice is now in ruins.

We sit in the garden of the old chateau-turned-restaurant, glad of the shade of the parasols. As we drink fresh coffee, a posse of three Dutchmen arrive on electric bikes. They ask us if we are going to Compostela and explain that they are on Day 24 of forty-eight of their pilgrimage from Holland to Compostela. I rather feel having electric bikes is cheating somewhat, but wisely refrain from voicing it.

Our route today once again takes us along a *Chemin de St-Jacques*, the Way of St James, and we follow the shell signs of the pilgrimage route as it heads upwards again, towards Santiago de Compostela. The grassy path soon turns into a mud slide for us to climb up and negotiate. It is thick, heavy, squelchy mud, infested with mosquitoes and smells; beside it are fields of white geese, large flocks resting under hedgerows, occasionally rising to flap their wings, and with strong scents of their excrement. It is not a pleasant walk, but the caffeine and the sugar are working their magic and we clamber bravely on. We struggle and slither and squelch and slide. It is exhausting at times. I think of those pilgrims again – perhaps walking barefoot, either because they could not afford sandals or because they had chosen to walk without foot coverings as a penance for their sins.

'Do you think it might be easier to walk barefoot through this?' I say, slithering along. 'Pilgrims wouldn't have had heavy backpacks either, to weigh them down. Perhaps travelling light has a lot to recommend it after all.'

A sign above an alabaster statue of St Jacques informs us that it is 540 kilometres back to Arles and 916 kilometres on to Santiago de Compostela. It reminds me that the mediaeval pilgrim not only had to walk *to* Compostela but had to then turn around and endure the walk home again, provided that he had even survived as far as the end. I am grateful for only having to go in one direction and be able to fly home. He wouldn't have known, when he first set off, whether he would ever see home and loved ones again. He had to have the blessing of his parish priest before leaving, and to have settled all quarrels and debts before receiving that blessing. The preparation and leaving might have been one of the hardest parts of the entire enterprise.

An Oddity

We sit in the grass at the corner of a field to eat the sandwiches purchased at the *boulangerie* in L'Isle-de-Noé and I remove my left boot. The foot is not happy, and my sixth toe is complaining. Yes, you did read that correctly. A deformity from birth, two little bones form a large bump at the side of my left foot, with two separate square nails, attached by webbing to the fourth toe; the extra width is now rubbing and the webbing has a tiny blister in between the toes. I rub some ointment in; it's impossible to dress it.

By mid-afternoon we are in the pretty hill-top town of Montesquiou. We sink gratefully into the old iron chairs on the terrace outside the bar and drink cool-ish beer and ice-cold water. We've only a further two kilometres to go so we can take our time, relax and enjoy this little respite. I Google Montesquiou and discover that it is named after the Montesquiou family, one branch of which is the d'Artagnan family. Robert Montesquiou apparently is famous for having been the inspiration for the Baron de Charlus in Proust's 'A la recherché du temps perdu.' And then there's the musketeer D'Artagnan too. A renowned family.

The helpful, friendly barman fetches a map to show us how to get to the house without going through deep mud, and shows us a shortcut that proves to be excellent. Again, we are grateful for local people who are friendly and helpful and go above and beyond what might be expected. They treat us kindly, not expecting anything in return, reaching out to proffer support where needed.

A Very Goose-y Farm

We are staying in the *chambres d'hôtes* wing of an old farm – a goose farm. It is surrounded by the sight, sound and smell of the geese. The converted wing is long and low and we enter through low double doors into a long room, filled with squashy sofas, and a vast table surrounded by chairs filling the length of the room. There is a staircase against one wall leading to bedrooms in the converted roof space, but there are two doors at the far end and one is ours. The room is modern, clean, with twin beds and a good-sized en-suite shower room. Best of all, it has French windows opening on to a small terrace and we wash our clothes and hang them out in the sun to dry. Then I take my journal and sit in the rose-covered round arbour on bright stripy cushions, with sun, a gentle breeze and several skitty lizards. Dinner is a fixed menu at 8pm; as ever, it's hard to wait so long when we are tired and hungry and longing to sleep. I nibble at the remains of yesterday's brioche to keep me going. I never thought I would eat brioche much, let alone be extraordinarily grateful for it!

Vente de Conserves d'Oies, the farm sign announced – the preserved goose products are sold direct to the public and indeed there is a big glass-fronted cupboard in the main living room, packed with jars and bottles and tins to purchase. So we should not have been surprised at the menu for dinner. There are six guests staying this evening; we are joined by the farmer and his wife at the long table, although Madame Marie-Grace pops up and down as she is cooking supper in the minute kitchen in the corner of the room. Monsieur arrives at 8.15pm and sits down next to me; I have Kim on my other side. Opposite us are the other two couples, one French, one Belgian, both of whom are touring the Gers. The Belgians are walking from Toulouse to Lourdes.

'We walk a lot, and do one longer walk each year,' they tell us. 'We use a tour operator that moves our luggage each day and we just have to walk the paths mapped out for us.'

It's what we have done several times in Italy, walking parts of the pilgrim Via Francigena, the old route from Canterbury to Rome, or from Todi to Assissi, or along the Amalfi coast. So we compare walking notes and are amazed when they tell us that he is 74, she 72; they look at least ten years younger than that and are fit and strong. Walking is good for you, we all agree. They have excellent English and also excellent French; the French couple can't speak any English, but convey to us that they are driving around the area for a few days. *Monsieur le Farmer* has the strong nasal accent of the region, and talks loudly and at length. Madame Marie-Grace says little and cooks a delicious meal – goose pâté de foie gras, fresh bread, green salad, rillettes, slices of melon, thin dried duck strips.

It's 8.45 pm before the main course is served – a delicious *magret d'oie* – roast goose breast, in a rich sauce, served with sautéed potatoes, yellow courgettes and masses of parsley. Monsieur is generous with the local red or white or rosé wine. It is all delicious but I am so tired I can barely eat. The conversation covers Brexit and goose and the Gers and walking. At least, I think it does; I can barely stay awake and my French deserts me. Eventually I switch off completely and when the dessert is served, I proffer my excuses and leave, heading for my bed and a good night of deep sleep. It was a prune clafoutis – I would have hesitated to eat it anyway, not wanting the effects of prunes while walking tomorrow.

Chapter Eight
Finding the Dream

Swallowing My Words

There's muesli for breakfast, and natural yoghurt, and cheese – and when I ask Madame for fruit she brings apples, bananas, pears, apricots. I have a feast without a single piece of bread or cake! The effect on my constitution is amazing. We are ready to leave by 8am – but then Kim has a feeling that he should just check the route, and discovers it's not quite right, and has to work it out again. And then decides to re-pack his things methodically and slowly. My impatience grows. I am ready to leave! I read a bit; go outside and clean my muddy boots; determine not to say anything. Over the past few years I have become so impatient and the quick vitriolic words have often spilled out unnecessarily, causing hurt to us both. Now, I bite back the impatient words and instead try to occupy myself with other things.

Why is it so easy to allow the harsh negative words to pour out of me – and so difficult to remember to offer love, praise, thanks? Sometimes, maybe even subconsciously, I'm thinking: well he deserves it; he's caused me so much pain over these past few years and no-one would blame me for being short tempered and saying things as they are.

And then I remember my marriage vows and how I promised – *promised!* – to have and to hold for better, for worse, in sickness and in health. He has been mentally ill, suffered a breakdown, not been himself in so many, many ways. A promise is a promise is a promise. And I've not been angelic myself for every moment of every day, I know. How to extend grace to others is a lesson I have continually to learn. It's so tempting and all too easy to be supercilious, assume oneself to be better than others. And so hard to have the humility of Christ.

> *Do nothing out of selfish ambition or vain conceit. Rather, in humility value others above yourselves, not looking to your own interests but each of you to the interests of the others. In your relationships with one another, have the same mindset as Christ Jesus: who, being in very nature God, did not consider equality with God something to be used to his own advantage; rather, he made himself nothing by taking the very nature of a servant, being made in human likeness. And being found in appearance as a man, he humbled himself by becoming obedient to death – even death on a cross!* (Philippians 2:3–8 NIV)

How to gain that mindset? Have the humility and grace and compassion I want extended to me, and extend it to others? *'Make me more like Jesus,'* I pray now. *'Give me the grace to forget my impatient words and to relax and not have to be in control.'*

It's 8.45am before we eventually leave, and now I am worried about the forecast hot temperatures. A very different worry after all the rain. However, we are in good heart, there's a spring in my step and we take the hills in our stride, marching along the road at a good pace. Today we will average 5 kilometres an hour, very different to the slow pace caused by mud and rain. My favourite walking socks have dried out at last, the new gel insoles are wonderful, and life feels very different. I apologise to my husband for yesterday's moaning and today's impatience.

I should swallow my impatient ungrateful words more often – they are non-fattening.

Living the Dream

The glorious deep-blue sky lit by the blazing sun makes me dig deep into my backpack and find the somewhat battered straw sun hat I haven't worn for nearly two weeks. We walk across sand-coloured farm tracks and suddenly there's a glimpse of the Pyrenees glinting on the horizon, not spotted for nearly two weeks. Life is suddenly good again; after the 59–63F of last week, we are reaching the mid-80s today. I love the warmth and the sun; my heart is happy. At mid-morning we stop for coffee by a little lake. Fish leap, frogs croak, there are a couple of pretty cottages reflected in the water. This is how I had imagined it would be: France in all her glory, happy hours of walking, blues skies, bright sun, time to stop for coffee from our flasks, kindly filled by Madame this morning.

Up above us is the fourteenth-century village of Bassoues, perched precariously on top of a steep green hill. We clamber up to discover a charmingly beautiful village. It's a *bastide,* a fortified mediaeval city. There's a severe fourteenth-century stone keep, part of the old castle of the Archbishop of Auchs; other turreted walls and *donjons* are half timbered, built of warm golden stone and ancient rough upright beams. The village is laid out on a long rectangular grid system, with a glorious sixteenth-century timber-covered marketplace running the length of the village and now housing the road through the middle. There are historic houses teetering along each side, many converted into cafés or restaurants or artists' studios.

Kim peers into the pottery; he loves to buy little things for me and until now we've not seen anything worth carrying; but this is pretty blues and creams and there is a tiny round dish which he proudly and lovingly presents to me, as I loiter outside to talk to the friendly tan-and-white spaniel lying in the sunshine. It is quite the most gorgeous village we have encountered so far – yet again! And we long to linger and explore. But today is a long day and we need to keep going. Out through the mediaeval gateway and we spot a little minimarket; it yields fruit, chocolate, ice-cold drinks. Then we're off again, striding along confidently, knowing that tomorrow is a rest day. We can do this!

Doing Nothing Mindfully

Walking along and thinking of nothing, the air fresh and invigorating, the scenery gloriously beautiful, the isolation and quietness feeding my soul. There is something about being out in nature and doing nothing – disguised as walking, for in our over-productive culture, we're not allowed to do nothing. My grandmother wasn't even sure about sitting down and reading during daylight hours; she felt one should always be 'doing something', because 'Satan finds work for idle hands to do' and she would tut at me when I curled up in an armchair with a favourite book. The Puritan work ethic.

Perhaps 'doing nothing' and mindfulness and the realisation that we need 'down time' are now much more accepted. And walking is therapeutic; the experts tell us that it really does make a physiological difference and improves our state of mind.

When I was suffering after witnessing my ninety-year-old mother run over and crushed by an out-of-control car, I was diagnosed with post-traumatic stress disorder (PTSD). I began seeing a therapist and she recommended EMDR for me – Eye Movement Desensitisation and Reprocessing – a form of psychotherapy in which the person recalls the distressing images while watching something moving from side to side – the therapist's finger or a dot on a machine. I was nervous about this process; it sounded like hypnotherapy to my uneducated mind. So I did a lot of research before being subjected to it, and discovered that Francine Shapiro, an American psychologist, had become aware of the effect rapid eye movement had on her own feelings when she was walking in a park, looking from side to side at the flowers and trees. The walking and the eye movement combined reduced the negative emotions and anxiety.

British psychiatrist, Jeremy Holmes, has also written about having counselling sessions outside and allowing patients to talk as they walk, and the effects this achieves. Freud, of course, used to take his clients out into the streets of Vienna to walk and talk. And it is now known that stress and anxiety cause high levels of cortisol in the body; the hormone is relieved by oxytocin, and that in turn is produced by walking in the fresh air. It's also produced by hugging, which is a rather lovely by-product of hugging! Walk and hug. Hug and walk. It's difficult to hug someone wearing a large cumbersome backpack; a quick arms-on-the-shoulders and a swift kiss will suffice for now.

So walking is good for you physically and emotionally, and spiritually too, for some of us. I find it much easier to pray and reflect and feel God when I am out in the countryside, walking and thinking and not doing very much except 'being' – being present in the moment, aware of my surroundings and looking around and enjoying the beauty of nature as I walk, with nothing else pressing on my agenda.

It can take a while to enter into this; walking day after day after day, as one does when on pilgrimage, means there is time to get used to it, to leave behind all the stress and the strain and the pressure of our everyday lives, to know that there is nothing else that has to be done – except walk.

It is very liberating and the warmth and the sun and the movement and the beauty lift my spirits. I am glad to be alive, glad to be walking, glad that this Great Walk is happening at long last.

What a difference sunshine and a good night's sleep make!

Another Rest Day Already

The GR route takes us over a ridge and then plunges down into a beautiful valley of fields – hay in its rows ready to be wrapped, hedges and copses, languorous cows. The mud has already dried in the sun and warmth and we cross the field, go through a gate on a farm track and come into a little courtyard beside a large pretty house with a terrace on the side. A big black-and-white collie leaps out at us and begins to bark – my hearts races – but she is friendly and it's a bark of greeting as she trots towards us, tail wagging, to welcome us to the Relais de Bastien, the remote family-owned and run hotel where we will spend the next thirty-six hours. This is it: we have arrived and tomorrow is Midsummer's Day and our rest day.

Madame comes to greet us, offers to do our washing (I am by now convinced we look and smell appalling) and shows us to the most delightful little blue-and-cream room up in the eaves, furnished with a large, comfortable bed, a delicate blue-and-cream painted desk by the tiny dormer window for me, a sofa for Kim on which to stretch out – and a kettle and cups and saucers and a mini fridge. It is delightfully charming. We don't have to do *anything* – except cross the lawn around the swimming pool and fall into a bubbling hot tub to soak away our aches and pains before lying on the wooden steamer chairs around the pool and soaking up some sun.

Later I dive into my backpack and find one of the two dresses I have brought with me for nicer evenings. One is an Indian-cotton, blue-and-white-paisley patterned v-neck; the other, a navy-and-white striped jersey dress. Neither crease and can be rolled up and stuffed into the bottom of the pack without detrimental effect. Now I can wear a nice dress with a little bling to brighten it – necklace and earrings bought fairly cheaply for the trip so that if they were lost or stolen it would not matter. They are a matching rose gold, with an aquamarine stone in the centre of a rose roundel. And makeup and mascara for the first time for three weeks. It suddenly looks artificial and mature (read old!) and less relaxed.

I am interested by how one's perceptions are so subtly altered in such a relatively short space of time.

Midsummer's Day

Midsummer's Day dawns grey and mizzling with low mist. Really? We potter up the road between the fields to stretch our legs after a long, late, leisurely breakfast; and we talk and share together, holding hands. Kim shares how planning this trip to fulfil my dream of the walk across France has been part of his trying to help put things right again between us, of demonstrating his love. It feels good and better and a huge robust step. I am grateful; and tell him how I am beginning to see him not as the person causing me pain in our marriage but once again as my knight in shining armour, who helps me and is leading me in the right direction and enabling us to do this together.

It is a very private and healing moment.

We repair to our room and I take advantage of the lovely desk and chair to read more extracts from the book of Exodus, to reflect, pray, journal, write. Chapters 13 to 19 were this week's daily readings; I'm doing them in one extended stretch and it gives a wonderful overview of a rather longer walk than ours – the Israelites were walking for forty years. It was a wilderness detour: God didn't lead them along the main road even though it was shorter; he led them in a roundabout way in order to transform them into the people he wanted them to be.

And I look back at my life and see where God has given me what seemed like the longer route and perplexing guidance at the time. Am I aware of God's Presence with me, leading me on? Time spent walking is time to reflect, to feel, to notice.

And what about the times when the Israelites wanted to turn back, return to their former life even though they were slaves; can I empathise with their frustrations and yet agree with Moses when he told them to stand still and watch what the Lord would do for them? We belong to him and he *will* fight for us (Exodus 14:14) and yet he said to Moses, '*You* do it!' So Moses stretched out his arm to divide the Red Sea – and God sent a wind to part the waters. How scary was it to walk across where there had just been deep water – and I think of the mud we had to contend with over the past two weeks and the fears and the exhaustion.

Can I see how God has helped, and does it turn my fear to faith and trust, as it did for the Israelites?

'*With your unfailing love you lead the people*' (Exodus 15:13 NLT). And their thanks turn to worship and song. How do I express my emotions, which are a result of what the Lord has done for me? But, like me, the Israelites soon slip from thanks and joy to disbelief. Where is the water when they are thirsty? Why can't God provide and why do they have to be in this stupid wilderness when they could have stayed in Egypt? Could they trust God in this situation? Could they be obedient?

And I am reminded of what I 'heard' God command me earlier this year – 'Fast from recriminations, feast on forgiveness.' How well am I doing? It's good to have a weekly review and check; a daily one might be even better, I realise. Keep short accounts with God and with one another, we were told at our marriage preparation session.

Pottering over to the washing line to retrieve the laundry, I discover it has gone; not only has Madame brought it in, she has beautifully folded it to present to me. Once again I am overwhelmed by the small kindnesses of people, by how well they treat us, how much they do for us: total strangers who can do so little for ourselves of the ordinary everyday things normally taken for granted. We are wandering aliens yet the kindness and hospitality has been exceptional everywhere we have been. My mind sees the many homeless who loiter on the streets of Bath, dishevelled and disorientated and deeply needy. How might I show them the love of God?

It's a thought I shelve for now, to return to once we are home.

Discovering Blanche

By the late afternoon, the sun has returned and it's summer again. The tables are set for dinner outside, sitting out on the little stone-flagged terrace under the trees, iron chairs at round tables. Madame says it's the first time they have used the terrace; usually from early May they can begin to sit out in the evenings but this year has been so wet and cool. So the tourists have not come and they are feeling the financial consequences of a poor summer. She brings us the house cocktail as an aperitif.

And I am hooked.

Gascony, this large yet remote area of deepest south-west France, is famous for three things: duck (especially foie gras), rugby and Armagnac. The local Armagnac is clear and potent – Blanche d'Armagnac, matured without oak so not amber in colour like the ones we are familiar with. I'm not sure what is in this 'house cocktail' other than the Blanche d'Armagnac, but it is absolutely addictive and we both accept the free refill. It goes well with the *hors d'oeuvre* of *foie gras de crustillade* – foie gras served in delicate thinnest puff pastry. And an *amuse-bouche* of scented cauliflower puree, decorated with blue borage flowers and served with the tiniest devils on horseback.

Two non-resident couples arrive for dinner: a married couple sitting behind Kim, and two sisters next to us. It is soon very obvious that we are all English and conversation flows delightfully. Angela and Jonathan are from the Channel Islands, and have had a house near here for some years. Angela is actually German but speaks excellent English, and Jonathan reveals that he is an actor and has appeared in TV episodes of both *Morse* and *Bergerac*, two series we have avidly watched over the years.

We refrain from telling him we don't recognise him.

The two sisters, Molly and Becky, also have a family home here – in nearby Plaisance. Becky has recently completed a three-day pilgrimage on the St Cuthbert Way to Holy Island and Lindisfarne, and she asks for details to sponsor our walk.

There's huge warmth and encouragement from everyone for what we are doing. It's another lovely evening, with special people, and we feel privileged to have this time to enjoy it. And today's walk was just how I imagined it would be – France in all her glory: warm, sunny, with gorgeous historic villages to pass through, and delightful places to stay with wonderful gastronomic delights.

We are truly living the dream!

Chapter Nine
Finding the Cure

Week three, Day 21, and it's the final part of the Great Walk across France. We are refreshed and revived after thirty-six hours of rest and we are raring to go again. Refilling the backpacks these days takes a few moments – a place for everything and everything in its place – and we are ready to go. It's cool and misty and damp as we leave the comfort of the *relais* and head up the little grey road to re-find civilisation and today's route. But a few kilometres further up the hill and the wonderful TOPO GPS on Kim's phone crashes completely. All data lost. Do we retrace our steps back to the hotel for Wi-Fi; or do we press on, hoping Kim can find the way to the next village?

KIM:
The maps I've planned only download by Wi-Fi; I have 4G so I could reload the normal map but not the map with the route planned out on it. Fortunately I could remember a little of the first part of the route so we headed onwards trusting that my memory was correct. But it meant a detour of a couple of kilometres into Beaumarchés in the hope of a café with free Wi-Fi. We had to spend some time there trying to decipher the Wi-Fi code, written in old-fashioned French

handwriting; even the woman behind the bar couldn't make it out. There were 24 letters: I or J? C or E? I was trying every possible interpretation and getting nowhere. The killer was that in the end what I thought was M was actually N. Eventually I retrieved all my data and maps from the Cloud and we were back on track. Huge relief.

The coffee was horrible, but the free Wi-Fi was a literally a God-send.

Walking sharply down on to the plain of the Adour River we are very aware of the effects of all the recent rains. We are following the course of the river, on our left, with fields of maize or corn on our right. There is mud and debris strewn around, covering the fields and the pathways; the lower part of plants and crops is coloured in pale-grey watermarks. A lot of the crop is tilted or already flattened; water lies at field edge. It is a dismal walk along a small back road, in the mist and low cloud, with the sad monotonous fields of maize stretching out in every direction. It's very strange after the rolling countryside of the Gers to come on to this flat plain. It's not perfectly flat; nor is it the sunken Fens; but it's fairly boring to walk kilometre after kilometre with no change of scenery, no change of height, nothing to challenge us. But it's easy walking, at least, and the pace is relatively fast – and that's a good thing as we have thirty kilometres to cover today. We are now heading towards Plaisance and our hopes are high – if it's nice enough for the sisters' family holiday home, it's probably a pretty town and might have some decent coffee. And *plaisance* translates as pleasantness. It beckons us on.

Unfortunately Plaisance turns out to be rather dowdy and dreary and down-at-heel. It does have a little *supermarché* and a square with a café. Re-caffeinated and restocked, we head on as the sun emerges from the clouds and the temperatures begin to climb. Butterflies flit, hydrangeas and hollyhocks have colour again, and tractors are ploughing up the destroyed crops and raising dust clouds. It all feels very different yet again.

A Delightful Place for Lunch

At lunchtime we begin to look for a spot to sit and relax; we are weary now and in need of a break. Kim recommends pushing on as there are lakes marked on the map and there could be benches by the side of the water. Even the thought of that spurs us onwards hopefully.

The reality is very different: gravel pits behind high electric fences, surrounded by large machinery. It's deserted industrialisation in a very French way.

We press on through the tiredness and hunger for two or three more kilometres, cross a river on an old stone bridge, and see down below us a wonderful tall solid picnic bench by the riverside, under shady trees. It's peaceful and practically perfect. The sun is burning off the clouds and the temperatures are rising again. Gratefully, I almost run down the track below the bridge and struggle out of my back pack, flinging it down as I sink on to the bench. We feast on *Tomme de Pyrenees* (a local cheese), chocolate, apples and fresh sweet apricots. We doze. Kim reads. I lie on my back and practise being a dead beetle.

Life is good; an hour of calm and rest and food revives us and we set off in renewed good spirits in warm sunshine.

From the Middle of Nowhere to the Edge of Nowhere

A signpost on the edge of town points to Pau and Bordeaux. We are emerging from the middle of nowhere to the edge of nowhere. A little over a hundred miles to go. There's excitement in the anticipation tinged with sadness that the end is in sight and soon we will have finished. Once upon a time, a walk of a mere one hundred miles was a huge undertaking. Now we are thinking, 'There's only a hundred miles still to go!' We need to learn not to look ahead, to live in the moment and enjoy this, now. To notice what is, be grateful for the gift of now, appreciate this time together and make the most of it.

It's sad to have left the beautiful rolling countryside of the Gers with its long inclines, views of the Pyrenees, trees, wheat fields. We're coming down to the Landes which goes all the way to the Atlantic. It was once a vast salt marsh, but Napoleon III needed pine trees for building his navy so the marsh was drained, and shepherds turned into foresters. It's now a land of forests and spa towns. And sandy beaches.

The part we are crossing first, though, is flat plains often lined with maize fields, many of which are higher than the roads, and we can't see over the green shiny-leaved maize. It forms a monotonous open tunnel. When we do see habitation, there are often many *tricoleur* flags defiantly fluttering – this is National Front territory. It's also rugby country – both *Quinze* and *Treize*, and there is much rugby talk and mention of Jonny Wilkinson, which brings an instant rapport with Kim.

This afternoon, we choose to take the small back road yet only see two cars in ninety minutes. The larger road, which is a slightly shorter route, can be seen on the horizon, with cars and lorries whizzing along. We feel justified in the choice of route. Soon we are on the edge of Riscle, tonight's accommodation town, and it's hot. The heat is reflecting up from the tarmac and we are feeling every bit of it.

The first thing we reach on the edge of the town is a large Carrefour *hypermarché*. 'We need a few essentials such as toothpaste and deodorant,' Kim says: the small travel sizes have died. 'We might as well shop here and see if they have cold drinks too.'

In we go and the air conditioning cools us down, and the cold drinks cabinet yields a celebratory beer for Kim and an iced green mint tea for me, to keep us going for another three kilometres through town.

KIM:
How to survive the final KILL-o-metre after walking 30 km today: stop at Carrefour and buy an ice-cold beer.

Sleeping in a Railway Station

Tonight we are staying at *La Gare*, the station. Kim finds the Avenue de la Gare on Google maps, and we walk through the suburbs – modern small French houses, straight roads, people staring at the unfamiliar sight of backpackers trudging through their neighbourhood. Eventually, at the very end of the very last road, we come to the old railway station: a long, low, creamy building set back behind head-high white level-crossing gates. It has been converted to a wonderfully quirky home and offers BnB.

Monsieur le Chef de Gare, the station commander, comes to meet us, rolls back the gates, and ushers us into the ticket office.

So begins the most delightful evening of wonderful eccentricity. Monsieur and Madame are from Paris. She is plump and jolly and bright and does all the work; he is thin and wiry and energetic.

'The locals think we have an accent,' she laughs. As far as we are concerned, their French is fabulous and easy to understand – no nasal twanging at all, just clear Parisian. 'My husband has been collecting railway ephemera for over fifty years and he wanted an old railway station to show it all off and display it. So when he retired four years ago, we searched all over for one to convert – and here we are!'

It's a wonderful conglomeration of his collection. Wherever you look there is train memorabilia, whether timetables and poster adverts framed on the wall, battered old suitcases piled up on the porter's hand trolley, waiting room chairs adorning the sitting room, or signposts directing you to the platforms. Madame decided that if he was going to play trains, she would do BnB; our room is the Orient Express, wonderfully over the top with purple and black and gilt furnishings, and opulent bedcovers. There is a *wagon-lit* sign on the door and a bathroom generous with lotions and potions. We relax, rinse out our clothes, and sit by the pool in the garden. Kim swims and discovers the Jacuzzi. There is a 60cm train track in the garden; there are chickens running around.

'Fresh eggs for breakfast,' Monsieur tell us as he shuts them up for the night. The late afternoon sky is clear dark blue; there's not a cloud in sight. I snooze on the sun lounger. And Jazz the Weimaraner comes to be patted; he is gorgeous – tall, pale-grey, affectionate and very quiet.

Dinner is on *Quai* 2, the original platform of this station, with its sloping roof sitting on ornate ironwork pillars; the station clock is correct at 7.30 as we are seated for dinner. Madame serves us her homemade deliciousness, while Monsieur sits inside, in front of the football on the television.

'He's Living the Dream,' she explains. Dessert is 'chocolate mousse *a la maison*'. It's a frothy dream of chocolate made with the fresh eggs.

There won't be eggs for breakfast after all.

Eccentricity

Next morning we are up, breakfasted, packed and ready to leave by 8am. It's a glorious morning. *M. et Mme la Gare* pose with Jazz at the azure station door for us to take their photo, standing under the blue-and-white sign proclaiming *Chef de Gare*. Kim takes a couple of steps towards the gate and feels something glutinously sticking underneath his boot. Little gravel stones are embedded in black tarmac in the ridges of the sole, the result of yesterday afternoon's hot temperatures. Monsieur and Kim retreat inside the little stone outhouse – it is obviously the man cave as the sign above the door says '*Hommes*'. It takes them a further twenty minutes to dig out all the solid debris, using various tools and implements.

'*Regardez!*' Monsieur warns us, 'watch where you walk. The tar melts in the heat.'

We bid them farewell again and stride off down the road. Kim suddenly remembers we haven't begun today by praying, so we stop and turn towards each other to hold hands. He happens to glance back towards the station and spots Monsieur and Madame watching us, taking photos of our receding backs.

Presumably they regard us as the eccentric ones.

A Strange Pilgrim

Today is a long day of walking, but with a wider variety of routes – grassy paths, an old railway bridge over the river, a road through a pretty village with its mediaeval covered wash area. The Pyrenees glisten on the distant horizon, the sun is wonderfully warm and everything feels great. Today I have an upbeat song in my head: 'One more step along the road I go.' Kim, walking behind me, sees me bouncing along at a good speed as my steps go in time to the tune. We're averaging over 5 kilometres an hour this morning.

As we emerge from the tree-lined pathway beside the railway track, we spot other walkers ahead of us on the open path through the fields – a pair, followed by two singletons. It causes us to increase our pace to see if we can catch up with them. Not that we are competitive or anything. We are soon following the route of the *Chemin de St-Jacques*, the route to Compostela from this part of France. Then one of the singletons turns aside to some old plastic chairs, to sit in the shade under the trees on the right. As we draw nearer we can see a table and information about the *Chemin de St-Jacques* and details of local hostels exclusively for pilgrims. The walker is a scruffy man in his late thirties, thin and wiry with long scraggy hair, wearing a red t-shirt, greying shorts and a black hat. He calls out to us, and I realise he is missing all his front teeth, upper and lower. He has a bulging red rucksack at his feet and a vast 'bag for life' beside him.

'*Bon jour!*' he says, beckoning us over to his chair. '*Vous êtes d'où?* – where are you from?' We tell him we are from England. 'Are you going to Compostela?' he asks. We exchange a few pleasantries, as his English is understandable, and he tells us he is walking the *chemin*.

'I 'ave a leetle fa-voure of you,' he says. 'I need just a couple of euros to 'ave enough for a bed tonight. So you 'ave per'aps two or three euros to spare?'

Kim hands over two euros, we wish each other *'bonne chemin'* and *'bonne continuation'*. We leave him sitting in the chair, never guessing we would spot him again later.

My left toes are beginning to hurt again and we have no coffee in our flasks today. There is a call for a detour into the nearest little town, and we wander around looking for somewhere which might serve coffee. A passer-by whom we ask points us to the *boulangerie* and the *épicierie* but alas neither offer coffee. It is a very strange town, bleak and dark; red brick on our left, with a modern open square to our right, edged with concrete blocks. The *épicierie* is an upmarket delicatessen with overpriced specialist cold drinks; the *boulangerie/pâtisserie* has very little choice so we settle on two *pain aux raisins*. Sitting on a concrete block in the shade, nibbling rather dry pastries, I notice that the house across the road from me is vacant – stripped back to bare brick and open holes, windows and doors gaping wide, overflowing with a multitude of pigeons. It looks grotesque and horrible and seems to sum up the feeling we have about this town. Cramming the last of the pastries into our mouths, we head out of town, glad to leave it behind, and on the outskirts come across a large Carrefour supermarket. A picnic lunch looks possible so we head in and make some purchases.

As we are packing the goodies into our rucksacks, the next customer comes to pay at the checkout immediately behind us. He is the 'pilgrim' we spoke to earlier and he is buying two immense plastic bottles of cheap wine, four cans of lager, and two long baguettes. It gives us a horrid feeling; he ignores us and we hurry out, not knowing what else to do.

Kim is rueful. 'I should have known not to give him cash,' he says. 'We never did in parish life when tramps came calling, always giving them food or taking them to buy whatever they needed, like a bus ticket and paying directly for it.'

'Do you remember the regular tramp in Stamford?' I reminisce. 'And how he turned up at lunchtime on Christmas Day expecting a plate of turkey with all the trimmings, and we were only just back from church and having a quick yet special lunch? He wasn't to know we would eat dinner in the evening but he was most put-out when I gave him a smoked salmon sandwich!'

Kim laughs. 'Yes, and the two in London who asked you for ham sandwiches on white bread *not* brown, and English breakfast tea, *not* Early Grey muck, as they called it!' Life in a vicarage is never dull.

The *Chemin St-Jacques* is clearly marked with shells and pointers set into the pavement; at pretty Aire-sur-l'Adour we part company, the route continuing to the left and into the town, but we are turning right and up the hill. We linger on the bridge across the river, enjoying a sunny moment over the sparkling water, the colourful flowers in window boxes, the cheerful crowds in a nearby bar and restaurant. As we head up the road leading us away from the town, a woman comes running after us, calling us.

'Do you know where you are going?' she asks us, breathlessly catching up with us as we pause. 'I saw your large backpacks – you are pilgrims going to Compostela? The *chemin* is back there – you have missed the turning. This is the wrong way!'

Yet again we are amazed at the kindness of strangers. Thanking her, we explain we are heading to the Cap Breton and the Atlantic. Her surprised face is a picture!

An Attitude of Gratitude

As we walk, we continue to talk – maybe the impressions gained on this momentous hike, or recounting things people have done to help us, or bouncing ideas around for our return to home and 'normal' life. Walking enables us to talk more freely and at greater depth than we do at other times; for some reason it's invigorating and inspiring to share as we walk, especially when the path is wide enough to be side by side.

'What still irks you about the new house?' Kim asks. We've lived there barely a year, and it doesn't yet feel quite like home. It was a house he found, and I hadn't wanted to move there at all. It was too far out of the centre of Bath; it was brand new – actually just a bare shell with no walls or floors inside and he designed the inside himself.

But I had wanted an old cottage, a south-facing garden, peace and quiet. Instead we have a modern house with a north-west facing courtyard and a busy little shop immediately opposite that attracts lorry drivers and walkers and cyclists and all sorts of passers-by. And which has been burgled several times, when we've heard the crowbars smashing the shops doors and windows in the early hours.

'What could we do to make the house feel more like home?' Kim says now, and I am struck again by how caring he really is and how often I take him for granted. And how ungrateful I am. We have a lovely house, everything works, it's warm and cosy and there's room for our family to stay – and they seem to like coming and come often.

I think about 'home' again. What does it mean for me? We have moved a lot in our married life, including a few years in the States. Everywhere we have lived I have tried to put down roots: to learn local history, to walk the area and discover as much as I can about it. I've unpacked and put precious things around me to make it feel homely. Even when we moved continents we took everything with us; we actually thought it was a forever move, and were surprised to find ourselves returning to England.

'Maybe I should think more about what I can be grateful for about the house,' I say slowly. 'It's convenient and easy to look after, and that includes the courtyard. It's easy to lock up and leave and that's good, particularly at the moment. And the shop is very useful, I have to admit.' We laugh about how often we pop across the road to what we have christened 'The Pantry'.

'Six times in one day is the record so far,' I admit. 'But that was when the grandchildren were here and they wanted to bake and I hadn't all the ingredients for what they were planning. And I was treating them to fresh croissants for breakfast too.'

I continue listing things that are good about the house and its location. 'I love the views from our bedroom right across the valley with the old houses below us; it's a gorgeous room.' And being grateful helps me to see it in a more positive way. I'm always amazed at how gratitude, even about things that seem on the surface to be painful or not what I want, can change the way I think about something.

'It will be good to go home after being homeless after all this time,' I say. Being on the road now and talking helps me to appreciate again what I normally take for granted. It has also shown me that actually I don't need very much at all. That having only two outfits to choose from each evening is strangely liberating; limiting choices makes it less stressful and far quicker! I think again about the Walk and how Kim has planned it and made my dream a reality. And yet again I pause to thank him and be grateful for the good things. Yet again I have to remind myself to concentrate on the positive and the good; and not dwell on the hurts and the pains and the negative things. Why is my fallback position that of remembering or looking at the bad? Why do I minimise the good or even forget it? Maybe it's time to start a daily gratitude list again; to daily remind myself in writing of three or four things about my husband for which I'm grateful or for which I love him. To allow myself to remember that wonderful young Cambridge oarsman with whom I fell in love, with whom I have had so much fun over the years, and who is the marvellous father to our three children. And who has provided a lovely home for us. I quicken my footsteps again. Maybe I want to get home sooner.

Planning Future Dates Together

'And what about us?' I wonder aloud. 'I love walking alongside you, doing this trip together. But how can we incorporate that into our normal lives?'

Kim thinks for a moment.

'We definitely should do more walking together,' he says. 'Maybe we should plan a longer walk once a week in the future. Time to walk and talk as we explore circular walks not too far from home. What about a Friday? It's a day we can each clear in our diaries, keep for a date day, maybe a pub lunch; time to continue what this long walk has brought us.'

'That's a great idea!' I enthuse. 'It would be time together, doing something we both enjoy. And already it feels like us against the world again. It always used to feel like that but I think we've lost the sense of it in recent years.'

We've become a team again and we want to take that feeling and sense back with us and continue to build on it. Planning it now, while we have the opportunity and the enthusiasm, means it is more likely to happen. We become excited by the thought of Friday walks. Now that we are retired, we can take a whole day to do that. But even as young marrieds with busy lives, we used to plan date nights even if they were at home due to smalls asleep upstairs, although to have a babysitter was ideal. Even if it was only an hour or two, it was time for us as a couple, to build into our marriage and have time together, maybe supper by candlelight, or a snuggle on the sofa together to watch a film, or play a board game. That precious time is all too easily squeezed out by busy lives unless we specifically put it into our diaries.

We need to begin dating again! Quite a thought for two sixty-somethings!

It is getting truly hot and the road seems never ending. There are no views as the fields are still higher than the road and the tall maize or sunflowers are blocking both vision and breeze. On and on we go, and my left foot is excruciating as we pound along the little road. Kim checks the map again.

Another Detour

'Oh NO!' he exclaims, 'we've missed the turning; we should have gone left back there!' He peruses the phone map, turns it around, considers the possibilities. 'We can take this detour; it's not a lot longer.'

But it is longer than it should have been, and my feet are burning now, and excruciatingly painful. I can barely feel my legs, and my right buttock has a painful twinge. I am literally limping along. This is definitely not fun.

At last the track appears and we can leave the road and head downwards. The coolness of a canopy of trees over our heads is pleasant, but it's a steep, rubbled track and I dislike going steeply down at the best of times. Today it is the final straw; the tears are flowing and I am scared that I will not be able to walk any further. I'm actually sobbing with pain and terror and the tears make it hard to see where I'm putting my feet.

'Nearly there,' Kim tries to encourage me. 'The detour only added a kilometre in the end, so it wasn't too bad.' But when you've already walked twenty-seven kilometres and have another five to go, every little counts. I am sidestepping down, leaning as much weight as I can on my pole, in so much pain with my left toes especially.

Taking the Cure

Eventually the track evens out and we spill out on to the pavement of the suburbs. We really are nearly there. Round another corner and before us lies the beautiful nineteenth-century spa town of Eugénie-les-Bains. The wide main street has pretty bunting strung between gorgeous old buildings which are painted in subdued but pretty shades of green and sage and pink and coral. The shops and the people are all 'upscale', as our American friends might say, and it looks very *gentil* and peaceful. Empress Eugénie de Montijo, Spanish-born wife of the French Emperor Napoleon III, used to come here to take the waters and the little town was built to accommodate others who copied her. Eugénie was the third and last Empress of France, and ended up living in exile. But her influence on the world of fashion lives on – Charles Worth designed 'modern' clothes for her and Louis Vuitton designed the trunks needed to transport the new bustled dresses.

We fall into the first outdoor café area, set back from the street on the edge of a little park with a stream running alongside. I sink on to a traditional metal chair, swinging my backpack on to the floor, and, the tears still flowing, reach down to unlace my boot and remove it. My foot goes up on to the next chair and I sit back and sob. In public!

Kim orders Lapsang tea and iced desserts, and then rummages in my bag for soothing foot cream for me to rub on my poor red, swollen feet. I don't care who sees; it's just such a relief to have my boots off. We manage to consume two mugs of tea, one beer, one coupe of passion fruit sorbet and two coupes of ice cream, and feel sufficiently revived to stagger on through the park to the hotel.

No guesses as to who consumed what!

He ties my boots to his pack and I find my soft espadrilles to stagger the final few metres to our hotel. There is a wonderful white line where my socks have been.

It is one of the cheaper spa hotels – there isn't a lot of choice other than spa hotels here as everyone comes to take the Spa Cure. This is a white building, set back below the road, with a separate building housing the restaurant. The receptionist is bright and cheerful in her white pseudo-medical coat, and shows us around: there are pools indoor and out, and there is a wonderful large Jacuzzi. It is not long before we are in it, having the pains and stress and tears bubbled and massaged away. I am feeling very much better and can scarcely believe that an hour ago I was sobbing in public, with my bare painful feet up on a chair.

We have booked a table for dinner in the restaurant; at reception there was a menu with *lapin,* rabbit, for the main course. Kim had been reassured that there was a traditional menu too – he doesn't do well with bunny stew; and that dinner is served from 7pm – 8.30pm. Oddly early for France.

That should have warned us of what might lie ahead.

A strong but not unpleasant aroma of fish greets us as we walk in through the door of the restaurant and already there are several other diners, mostly older couples but also several single women at individual tables. The room is pleasantly decorated in white and cream and grey and beige – soft and relaxing. We are shown to a table for two, laid with a crisp white tablecloth, and we wait for the menu.

'Maybe I will have fish tonight,' Kim says. 'It smells quite nice.' He has his back to the room; I meanwhile am looking out across the restaurant and can see that everyone else is eating the same thing; it looks like a square lump of greyish white fish. And that it comes out ready plated. As we are contemplating what it might be, the young blonde waitress arrives at our table and plonks down the appetiser – plates of white tabbouleh topped with chopped tomatoes.

'*Non, non, le menu s'il vous plaît,*' Kim says.

'*Pas de menu* – there's no menu!' The waitress shakes her head. The look on Kim's face – he is absolutely horrified and stares blankly at her, unbelief mingled with shock. He gesticulates at the white food currently in front of him.

'I can't eat that!' He doesn't like healthy food at the best of times.

'*C'est la cure de santé,*' explains the waitress impatiently. 'It's the Health Cure.' More shock and horror from Kim's eyes. 'Everyone is here for the Cure; it takes three weeks of this special menu for

189

it to work,' she adds helpfully. Kim looks at me in despair and I can only imagine what is going through his mind. And what he might possibly do with this plate of food unless something else is available.

Maybe rabbit wasn't such a bad option after all. But there's no sign of it in here.

Kim sighs theatrically, turns back to the waitress and explains very slowly and sweetly in his best French that we have walked over thirty kilometres today, and are walking across France and we are very hungry and could we please have a menu and some wine? The waitress is impressed, and visibly softens towards us.

'*Attendez!*' she tell us; wait. And she removes the offending plates and disappears into the kitchen. Moments later she returns. '*M. le Chef* would like to know if you could possibly eat a little melon with port, perhaps a *magret de canard* with dauphinois potatoes and timbale of courgettes, and maybe a little dessert? And would Gascony white wine be all right?'

It turns out to be absolutely delicious, freshly prepared and cooked, and is eyed enviously by those around us. The fragrance of our meal must have been tantalising. While everyone else eats their pale, insubstantial, curative food, we tuck into vast portions of succulent dishes and Kim vows he is never coming to take the Cure. It is all very funny and causes us much mirth; Kim's horrified face was certainly a picture to behold. We are soon trying to stifle our giggles in this quiet and restorative curative place. We are even offered coffee, which no one else is offered; they all leave after a slice of beige pudding.

'Hard to know without a menu what the cost of this dinner will be,' Kim laughs, 'but frankly I'm not worried. I'm just so relieved to have had something other than that grey mess!'

It has been our longest day. I post about it on social media and a friend sends me a cartoon of Peanuts carrying Snoopy on his back, with the words, 'It's not where you go, it's who you travel with.'

'So let Kim carry you,' she advises.

'Keep going, Mum,' texts our son. Kim replies, 'It's only 5 more days, if I can nurse your mother along.'

I look up Eugénie-les-Bains on the internet and discover that it's known as the 'slimming village' and has become more famous due to the celebrated Michelin-starred chef, Michel Guérard, who has devised a special range of slimming menus, to be used by those who come to sample the water from the Empress spring. There are other springs too, but this particular one has a temperature of 19 degrees, and has been 'adapted' for the treatment of digestive disorders and for helping to regulate metabolisms.

Not the place for hungry backpackers then.

We sleep long and deep, not setting an alarm so that we can be truly rested and restored. Eugénie-les-Bains is working its magic on us – it's renowned for being a place of *tranquillité*.

Chapter Ten
Finding Fiesta Fun

Breakfast in the main house is a dismal affair. We are the only ones there at 8am and we assume that as it's been out and available since 5am, everyone else has breakfasted much earlier and gone to their treatments. A small, plump, dark-haired woman brings us each a little tray with a glass dish of tinned fruit salad, a wineglass of thickly sweet orange juice, and a wrapped croissant. There is a dull coffee machine in the corner of the room. We are not tempted to linger. I soon have Tiger Balm and toe caps as topical treatment, different socks and insoles for a change, and feel more able to cope today.

'Congratulations,' beams my Apple watch, 'you set a personal best yesterday of 1203 calories burnt in one day. Keep it going today!'

Nothing Lasts Forever

But it's a stroll in the park today in comparison with yesterday – a mere nineteen kilometres. I am coming to realise that anything I've had to endure on this walk is not forever. Long days, painful feet, thick mud, have each been a part of the experience and will be a part of the recounting and remembering of the adventure. We've had different beds just about every night, of very varying degrees of comfort and civilisation ranging from luxurious to weird. It's been endurable because we knew it was only for a moment. It's caused us to laugh and to laugh together, and has been a part of the whole experience. Is that something we could apply to everyday life too? To realise that even the most dreadful things can be regarded as part of the journey, something we are moving through. And that I am not defined by the weirdness and the difficulties. But they may help to shape me and make me stronger. I've lived through some exceptionally painful things in my life; and I have survived. And here I am, walking across France.

This morning our joints are talking to us, and the exertions of the two days of thirty kilometres each have taken their toll. And oh joy, we soon come to a hill. It means a change of muscles and stride and we actually both appreciate it after the miles and miles of flatness. Our hearts and lungs are certainly fitter than they were three weeks ago; but other parts of the old body are beginning to complain.

Only One Hundred Miles

A text comes through; it's late Sunday morning and our families are at home.

'William would like to know how many miles you have left to walk. This may be something you'd rather not think about . . .' writes our son on behalf of our grandson.

Kim stops to check. It was just the right time to do so – how did Will know?

We are *exactly* at the one-hundred-miles-to-go mark! Counting down in double figures from now on. And we can count on one hand the number of days still remaining. ONLY one hundred miles? It doesn't seem that much after what we've walked so far.

There is a danger in looking ahead to the end; there is a balance between striving for the goal and enjoying the pathway to get there. We have been walking into the unknown, with its challenges and adventures and disasters and joys. There are still a few days to experience the adrenaline rush, not knowing what each day holds or what lies ahead. It's been an adventure in trusting God and believing his promises.

'You show me the path of life. In your presence there is fullness of joy.' (Psalm 16:11)

Walking is in reality a slow process; it's a stepping aside from the rat race of life where we are hurtling towards some goal of our own making, with sideways glances to see if others are overtaking us. And then the journey becomes more about safely navigating the madness of the fast lane than enjoying the route we are travelling, whereas this daily walking has given time for looking around, taking in the beauty and appreciating the rhythm of a slower pace of life. I'm no longer following other people, wanting either to be on the same path and envying them their fast journey; or being distracted by their journey and forgetting the pathway God has for me.

What if this is how we are intended to live – trusting him to lead us into the unknown at a pace set by him, maybe taking longer than we had intended as he patiently gives us time to learn lessons that otherwise we would have rushed past? And can I trust Him enough to believe that my journey isn't going to end where sand meets water, that there is yet more even though I am in the adolescence of old age? That I can trust him to continue to lead me into what is, for me, the unknown? Can I relinquish control of the satnav to him? I have always liked to be in control but maybe that has been at the cost of robbing me of delights God wanted me to experience.

A Special Coffee

We are back to a speed of five kilometres an hour, passing through tiny hamlets, glimpsing the Pyrenees on our left on the blue horizon. Coffee is elusive. Eventually, coming up a hill to the crossroads in the centre of a village, I spot a young man unloading his shopping from the boot of his car. Bravely I approach and ask in French if there is anywhere to have coffee locally.

'Alas, no longer,' he replies. 'The café and the bar have both closed some years ago.' He stands and looks at me. Do I look as bad as I fear? Maybe not, for then he says, 'But we can give you coffee. Or a cold drink. Please – come into the kitchen.'

And he opens the double doors leading into the ultra-modern kitchen where his young wife is putting away their groceries. He proceeds to make us coffee while she goes to check on their toddler who has just been put down for a nap. He asks where we are from, and the response is the usual: 'Ah, *Bartt . . . Le rugby?*' And soon he and Kim are discussing rugby and Jonny Wilkinson and Bath rugby. This young couple have welcomed total strangers into their home, and it feels such a blessing and a privilege. It's a story we will recount many times to others, still wondering in amazement at this kindness to the wandering passer-by. We leave with a spring in our steps.

I hadn't liked to ask to use the cloakroom.

Today is a complete contrast to yesterday. The walk, the views, the kindness of strangers are all so very different to yesterday with its depressingly long roads, lack of views, and underhanded 'pilgrim'.

La Fiesta

This afternoon we are heading to the town of St Sever and I want to see its twelfth-century Benedictine abbey as it was modelled on the abbey at Cluny. It unusually has seven apses and is a UNESCO World Heritage Site. I am excited – I love old churches.

Kim has booked BnB in a rather lovely looking old house; Madame has assured him we can arrive from 3pm, and she will provide dinner as she is a good cook. We arrive to find St Sever in full carnival mode – there is a very loud, gaily coloured modern funfair opposite the house, taking up most of the street and filling the air with loud thumping. The house is deserted; so we hide our packs around the side of the house in the long undergrowth and set off to explore.

The centre of town is heaving with people dressed in costumes; bright blue or red or yellow bandanas adorn their necks, and there is a wonderful air of frivolity and fun. We manage to find a couple of seats on a bench at a long table on the pavement outside a bar and Kim pushes through the crowds to order cold drinks. A happy group of cheerleaders wearing vast purple wigs is dancing and frolicking along the road. As they draw closer it becomes apparent that they are rather large men in fancy dress. We think.

It's all rather crazy, underlined by the shop fronts being boarded up and moveable *pissoirs* being available every few hundred yards. The abbey sadly is also locked. Whatever else is expected during the carnival, it's not a spiritual experience.

Wandering around, I find another old church with a side door opening into beautiful mediaeval cloisters. No longer in ecclesiastical use, it is hosting a rather smart black-tie affair. Canapés and champagne are being served in the cloisters and

197

the main church is laid out with round white-clothed tables and sparkling glasses, and chairs covered in white with a large pink bow on each chair back. It looks so inviting.

'Can we pretend we are part of it?' Kim asks. I point out that we are not really inconspicuously attired in our walking clothes, so we take a quick look around and beat a hasty retreat.

There are old garden chairs on the lawn under the low spreading chestnut tree in front of the house where we are staying and we sprawl languorously in the heat. Kim tries phoning Madame, to no avail. The fun-fair noise is increasing. Eventually we get up and wander around to the back of the house, exploring the pool area and the gracious colonnades of climbing roses and the stone-flagged terrace running the length of the old house. Kim tries the back door; it's unlocked and he goes in, calling, and a dog begins to bark. He quickly retreats but a face appears at an upstairs window. An elderly lady seems to have been woken from her siesta by the dog barking. Guests, we call up to her. No, she doesn't know anything about that, but thinks Madame is at the festival.

Eventually Madame does turn up, two hours later than promised, but she is very sweet, tall and elegantly slim and grand, with upswept pale-grey hair. She speaks excellent English and is very apologetic, in a ditzy kind of way. Oh, and our room isn't ready and hasn't been cleaned because the Spaniards were staying for the festival and were meant to go today but have left their things in the room. And she will bring us beer and water if we will sit on the terrace while she gets it ready for us. So we sit and enjoy the large gracious gardens; the old house has a peaceful ambience and I think we snooze.

It's nearly 6pm before we are finally led up the old oak grand staircase, and up again to the second floor and two interlinked rooms at the back of the house. The first room has a single sleigh bed lavishly made up with beautiful white antique linens, walls lined with books in several languages, an old fireplace across one corner, a sofa in front of the balcony window. It's beautiful. And a door to the second smaller room, which has a small double sleigh bed, with a high foot board; and a magnificent old swinging cradle. Then we are shown to the bathroom – it is along the corridor, across a nursery school room of books and tables and chairs. Kim looks bewildered.

'It's not the room I booked,' he explains to me. We return to the bedrooms. 'Madame, I booked a pretty blue-and-white room with a four-poster bed and en suite bathroom. What has happened?' he says to her.

'*Alors*, alas,' she replies without missing a beat, 'the lady who was in there last night has decided to stay another night. And I can't move her.'

Kim is disappointed – he had planned a romantic stay in a gorgeous room with a bed without a footboard. He won't sleep well in a small sleigh bed in a cramped position. But Madame refuses to move us or to budge and suggests that I sleep in the single bed and he sleeps across the double bed. He asks about timing of dinner.

'Dinner?' she asks, looking blankly at him. 'There's no dinner here tonight. We are all out at a festival event. You didn't ask for dinner.'

'I thought I did,' he replies, 'when I booked the blue-and-white four-poster bed and we emailed about it all.'

She waves her hands airily. 'It's the fiesta! You'll easily find something to eat. Try the main square about eight or eight-thirty tonight. And be glad I've put you in this room – it's at the back and will be less noisy. The four-poster room is at the front and it's the last night of the fiesta and the noise will be horrendous until about two a.m.' And she's off. Kim is sadly resigned and I go to run him a bath in the vast bathroom and tip half the bottle of the liquid hand soap into the water to make lots of bubbles.

Wandering around the town later, it feels quieter than earlier. There are a few young families with buggies and balloons and candy; teenagers already the worse for wear. Not much is happening – it's the lull before the storm. The main square is deserted, its shops boarded up, the vast ancient Benedictine abbey still firmly locked. The pop-up food vans smell greasy and offer *frites* and hamburgers and not much else.

A Spanish Affair

Eventually we turn in under an archway on a side alleyway, the sound of a flamenco guitar drawing us in. It's a Spanish bar, complete with bull fighting on the television in the first low-ceilinged taproom, guitars propped up on a little stage in the back courtyard, and cooking going on at the far end under the command of an older woman. It's the start of an unexpectedly fun evening. We talk to the lady chef, who explains the evening timings and opens a bottle of Spanish wine for us. We people-watch – they are beginning to drift in; TV watch – the bull fight is strangely mesmerising; music watch – there's now a little band practising. At 7.30 the cold tapas are ready and we are served ham and cheese on disposable white plates; it looks just like our lunch earlier today. But the taste is divine – Spanish air-dried ham, delicious Basque cheeses. At 8pm, the platefuls of hot tapas get passed around. Fried chopped potatoes, brochettes of four different types of duck. We recognise foie gras and *magret*, but would perhaps rather not know what the other two indeterminate ones are. A young family arrive and perch around a tall barrel to eat. The two little boys, aged maybe seven and five, sport blue shirts with red bandanas; the older one is thoughtful and quiet, the younger one full of beans and wielding a toy sword with which he whacks his brother, his mother, his father. He is fascinated by the ukulele player and stands watching for ages.

By 9pm there's still not much happening; it's only just warming up. Kim wants a dessert and an Armagnac so we wander around again and realise that everything is about to open up and get going. He buys a sweet *crêpe* from a popup van and we potter back through the attractive old town, its beauty somewhat marred by funfair and festival. We are by now too tired to enjoy the fun, and we retire to bed and try to sleep. But as Madame predicted, it's a noisy night; it's hot and the music thumps and my foot hurts. Sleep eludes me.

Chapter Eleven
Finding a Green Freedom

A delicious breakfast is served outside under the pergola, in the early morning sunshine, dew on the grass, the sky cloudless and deep. We explain to Madame that tonight's hostess is collecting our backpacks later this morning. Today we will walk unencumbered. It is a strange feeling – we are definitely missing something! We leave the luggage by the front door and are on the road by 8am. The streets have already been swept and washed and it smells fresh and clean if slightly disinfected. And then we are out into the countryside and on to the *Voie Verte*, the Green Way, a wide old railway line that some fifteen years ago was made into a track for walkers, cyclists, horses. It's softer underfoot and we delight in the silky feeling, the green path and shade of the trees. There are pretty views – not stunning, but pleasant – across the plain, whenever there is a parting in the trees; and we stride along, passing underneath the walls of an old fortified town, crossing a little stream, enjoying the abundant blue hydrangeas growing on the old railway banks. The poppies and spring flowers of the earlier days of the Great Walk are long gone; hydrangeas and hollyhocks and roses are in full bloom.

Too Much Ice Cream

Sitting on a bench in the sun enjoying coffee, Kim leaves his phone lying beside him. By the time he picks it up again it has died, leaving a message: *This iPhone is too hot – danger. Do not use until it has cooled down.* So he takes it into the shade and they both enjoy a cooling siesta.

Later, the path detours through the edges of a small town and right past a little Carrefour.

'I need an ice cream!' declares Kim and in we go. A box of six mini Magnums is the cheapest way, and Kim eats the first one while standing in the queue to pay and by the time I'm paying he's on to the second. We stand in the coolness of the store for his third and my first, and then offer the two spare ones to everyone. They each refuse: the cashier isn't allowed to eat on duty, two people paying for their groceries tell us it's bad for the figure. We go outside and offer one to a man just leaving his car to go inside, and he looks askance and says a definite *Non!* In the end we have to throw the spares in the bin. I've also bought a large quantity of the chilled green mint tea concoction, and fill my water bottles with it. It's thirst-quenching, delicious and energising.

By this stage I am again becoming worried about my left foot, and the end three of my six toes. The whole area is so painful I am beginning to limp, especially after a rest when it takes a while to get going again. I'm worried I may be doing some permanent damage. Investigation reveals that part of the small webbing between toes four and five now has a tiny fissure as well as a blister. I rub in some painkilling antiseptic ointment and cover the other blister on the outside of toe six. There's not much else I can do. A plaster or blister dressing won't fit on the in-between part.

Closed on Mondays

Madame Eva lives at the end of a long driveway lined with glorious blue hydrangeas. The old white farmhouse is L-shaped with a red-tiled roof and French-blue shutters. There's a wide, open grassy courtyard with a palm tree in the middle; two little spaniels, one black and white, one tan and white, lie in the shade. Eva hurries out to meet us, brings us homemade lemonade to drink while we rest and cool off. A stately Dutchwoman, blonde and welcoming, born in the Hague, she left Holland at eighteen, moved to Cambridge and learnt English before going to cookery school in Lausanne and working in Switzerland for eighteen years. But she always dreamed of having her own hotel and restaurant and so twenty-one years ago she moved here to the south-west of France, and bought and renovated this *Domaine*. The two-sided house is the hotel; the barn forming the third side of the courtyard is the restaurant. And it is all closed today as it's Monday. We remonstrate that she has not only taken us in but also collected our luggage on her day off, and she laughs and says this year business is non-existent mostly due to the bad weather, and it is good to have something to do. And could she do our laundry for us? She whisks it away and before long I see it blowing in the breeze in the sunshine.

Later we have dinner at a table with a dark-red cloth under the matching parasol in a corner of the garden, and begin with a glass of delicious chilled Floc de Gascogne, a local aperitif of one third Armagnac and two thirds wine. It's heady with the scent of flowers. Eva explains how an aperitif of Floc is a local custom dating back to the sixteenth century, and that pure Floc must have wine and brandy from the same vineyards.

Later, Kim tenderly treats my blisters for me. I am tearfully grateful.

* * * *

Scrambled eggs for breakfast is a treat. So is Eva's open car boot door.

'Where are you heading?' she asks. 'I'll take your packs as I have to go shopping today.'

As we walk, unencumbered again, up the hill out of the village, the little blue car whizzes past and honks at us and Eva waves cheerfully.

'We could have accompanied the luggage,' I say somewhat wistfully. 'I always fancied being a bag lady!'

'No *trichee*!' Kim says, and we stride on remembering Clémence.

A Change of Atmosphere

A brief glimpse of the spectacular Pyrenees and then we plunge down into the valley and pick up the *Voie Verte* again. It's shady under the trees, soft to walk on, flat; by coffee time we are halfway, having left at 8.30am. It's easy walking, especially with no heavy packs. We pass a jogger, a couple of dog walkers, field after field of maize, go through a long brick tunnel where we enjoy hooting and whistling to hear the echoes. The green banks are laden with hydrangeas, their enormous flower heads in all shades of blues and dark purples. At Hinx, there is another little Carrefour supermarket – more green mint tea, cheese and fruit for lunch, an almond croissant for elevenses.

At the end of the *Voie Verte* we feel a change in the atmosphere, a thick silence, clearer air, the scent of pine trees as we head deeper into Napoleon's forest. The sea is less than fifty kilometres away. Can we sense it? It inspires us on. No longer just trying to keep putting one foot in front of another, we are determined to get there, blisters and pain notwithstanding. Only two days still to walk. And our thoughts begin to turn to dates and diaries for when we are home again, and we remember back to rain and mud, hills and spring flowers, cool days and sunburn; laughs we have shared and the sense of being in this together. We walk along hand-in-hand, feeling closer than we have for a very long time, until it gets too hot and sticky.

Walking has been therapeutic for us in so many ways, not least in our marriage. Being outside day after day in the beauty of creation uplifts the soul, untangles the mind, lessens anxiety. Changing the way we behave towards one another because of changing our movements. Taking on a challenge together has spawned new ways of thinking about each other, inspired creativity, made us more grateful for one another.

Academic experts have proved more than once that walking increases creativity and problem-solving abilities, lessens stress and anxiety, and relieves many of the issues facing our sedentary twenty-first-century lives. Plato and Aristotle said the same two thousand years ago. Of course, choosing the right companion is essential; either that or you walk alone and, although I do that a lot at home on my regular long hikes, I am glad to have had my best friend as my companion on this walk across France.

Another Alsatian

Kim's maps show that there is a green route continuing straight ahead even though the official *Voie Verte* has ended. We decide to keep going as it is shorter and more pleasant than taking the road. The path gradually narrows and becomes more overgrown until it ends at an electric fence, with notices saying '*privée*', and a dishevelled farmyard, with barns housing tractors and cows and farm implements.

'We'll have to go back,' I lament, but Kim checks the map again.

'It definitely marks a path through here,' he says. 'We can climb over and go through the farmyard – look, there's a road just the other side.'

'But there might be guard dogs,' I warn. It's a risk he thinks worth taking as he never ever gives up nor turns back.

So we scramble over possibly electrified fences, slip under wires, squelch through the farmyard mud and go around the modern farmhouse and out on to the road. And all the while I think of fierce French farmers with guns and ferocious guard dogs. My heart is racing with fear and terror. Kim stops to check the map again and I glance back across the farmyard. Lying in the shade of the nearside of the house is an untethered German Shepherd dog, his ears pricked. We had walked straight past him. I'm still sweating profusely with fear and the dog gazes straight at me.

Will he chase us?

But all is well, he is too hot to stir and we march on to Narosse where there are benches in the shade of the church and lavender bushes in full bloom with bees and tiny humming birds to keep us company as we eat lunch. Pine trees surround us: we are on the coastal plain of the former salt marshes. A month ago we were in the wild pale flowers of spring, followed by bright poppies and white marguerites. Now there are huge heads of hydrangeas in every shade of blue and mauve, window boxes of trailing pink geraniums, plump luscious apricots and blazing sun. Four weeks have made a significant difference in nature and in us.

Being Touristy

Five kilometres through the outlying suburbs of Dax bring us to our hotel – it's a cross between a carless motel and a hostel;

we have an access code and can enter at any time. Upstairs we find our room number, use another access code and we're into a tiny twin room overlooking tenements; and are greeted by our backpacks. Thank you, Eva! There is a tiny en suite shower (if you can squeeze in) and a little balcony on which to hang our clothes to dry. Everything we need. We've arrived in plenty of time to explore Dax, even after a shower and a siesta. Bliss.

Dax is just like our beloved home town of Bath – much loved by the Romans who built baths over the hot thermal waters, a tradition carried on by the Georgians, and today there are spas and places to take Le Cure with the mud from the thermal waters. We wander around the old narrow streets, dressed in summer clothes, enjoying being 'normal' tourists, stopping to sip a cup of tea in a delightful *salon de thé*, tea shop; poking into little antique shops and clothes shops and stationery shops. In the centre is the edifice of columns and statues and walls and fountains built over the hot water: *Le Source de la Nehe*, announces a sign over the arches, *Sulfatée Calcique*. Carved lion heads disgorge the water into troughs and I run down the shallow steps and dip my poorly toes in to the spa water in the hopes of healing. I hadn't realised just how hot water is when it's 64C. Ouch. Apparently it is good for treating rheumatism, due to the mineral and vegetable algae in the waters, which is why the Roman Emperor Augustus brought his daughter Julia here.

Then there's the statue of Jena-Charles de Borda, born here in Dax in 1733; he was a marine engineer and mathematician who helped to formulate the metric system. I drag Kim to view the house designed by Frank Lloyd Wright, which has one façade composed totally of plate glass. He's a bit more interested in that – we visited Lloyd Wright's home last year in the USA and found it bizarrely interesting. The best thing about Dax for Kim, though, is the artisanal ice cream. He pours over the displays of gorgeously exotic flavours and settles on a mixture of a coffee *boule* and a pomegranate *boule*. We perch on a low wall in one of the squares devouring its cooling deliciousness. Yes, I know it was he who bought an artisanal ice cream; but he did say I could have a lick or three . . .

By 6.30pm it's still registering 89F as we wander around in search of somewhere to eat. It's warm enough to sit outside and enjoy a duck salad and a local rosé wine.

The heat continues overnight; there's no air conditioning and so sleep is somewhat difficult. We are slightly jaded the next morning – and after two days without packs, unused to walking fully loaded. Orange juice freshly squeezed in the squeeze-your-own machine in Carrefour, *gros cafés* in the *boulangerie*, and we are recharged and refreshed, ready for what may lie ahead. The route goes through the old town and up on what is called the Balcony of the Adour River. We're excited to be walking alongside the river for a little way, until the footpath on the road gives out and we are walking on the busy main road leading in and out of Dax and sharing the space with the constant fast cars.

It is terrifying.

It is also rush hour.

Perhaps leaving early is not always the best idea. This is the most terrifying walking we have done so far and the prayers for safety this morning are soon repeated. The cars seemingly make no concessions for walkers; why should they, walkers are probably not normally encouraged to be along here and it is a main road after all. The traffic is pouring into Dax on this busy thoroughfare;

cars, coaches, lorries and motorbikes all screech past us and we try to squeeze against the hedgerows.

Tree Climbing

It's a little way until we can leave the main road and rejoin the river and we assume that our troubles will now be over. In fact they are about to get worse, if different. The recent rains have caused deep flooding, and the path is often submerged. The footpath is overgrown and the long grass adds to the difficulty. The high humidity brings out the flies and the mosquitoes. I find the anti-bug spray and we cover ourselves in the horrid-smelling stuff, although to little or no avail. Kim is in shorts and his legs are soon covered in bites.

Then we come across an enormous tree toppled completely across the path. Even lying sideways it is of significant height. I slip off my backpack and slide underneath through a tiny space, pulling my pack after me. Kim with his great height decides he can't get low enough to go underneath so he opts for climbing up and over – with his backpack on. And gets stuck at the top. He is rigid with fear, but I assume he's teasing and playing around, and I start laughing.

He is most offended and also slightly scared. He does not like heights at the best of times and now he is stuck with a heavy backpack and he freezes in terror. I have to climb up a little way and undo his straps and wriggle the pack off his back, throwing it down to the ground, and then help him negotiate a way down.

I find the whole episode rather funny; he later describes it as a nightmare and his worst moment of the entire walk.

Stuck in the Mud

The path disintegrates into more mud, more long grass, more non-navigable wilderness thick with mosquitoes. It's horrible to walk through, and Kim finds an alternative route, one that takes us across a nature reserve. It proves to be a much easier, flat walk, on small banks above the drainage ditches of the marshland. There are horses of a glorious rich chestnut with pale-cream manes and tails; water lilies flowering on the still water below us; oceans of a pretty yellow flower. Later we read a sign informing us that *La Jusse*, the yellow flower, is invasive, takes all the oxygen and is asphyxiating the fish.

A gateway takes us on to a slightly stonier path across a vast field. To our left, some distance away, is an old red Renault with an elderly gentleman shouting at us, waving us to come nearer. We are confused; but he limps awkwardly towards us, leaning on his stick. We can't make out what he is saying but he seems very perturbed so I head towards him. His accent is thick and he is obviously very upset but eventually he makes us understand that his car is stuck in the mud and he has no mobile phone. Might we call his wife and ask her to call the local farmer to bring his tractor to haul him out?

And this poor elderly gentleman, in his eighties, I guess, small, plump and dressed in ancient much-worn farming clothes, looks so woebegone and lost that Kim hands over his mobile phone. And then mine. But alas, neither of us has sufficient reception here to connect the call. We promise that when we get to Saubusse we will tell someone that M. Nugré is stuck in the mud and we leave him hobbling back to his car. A little further along there are two young girls walking towards us, deep in conversation, and we stop and tell them about M. Nugré and point to his car. They have mobile phones that work and they promise to go and talk to him; we look back a little while later and see them with him. We hope very much that someone comes soon to tow his car away – he is understandably beginning to get very worked up about it all.

'Why did he drive his car all the way out here when it's so muddy,' Kim wonders.

Formule or Nothing

It's given us something else to think about and to take our minds off the struggles of the day. The smelly mud, the humidity, the mosquitoes and the heavy backpacks are unsettling us. My left foot is painful; Kim's legs don't feel right. Just one more day, we encourage each other, we are so very nearly there. And we walk up into the village of Saubusse anticipating lunch. It proves to be a village of much-faded splendour. The first building encountered is a grand nineteenth-century house, once a splendid hotel for those who came to sample the spa waters here, but now shuttered and empty; the church is immense and dark and brooding, covered totally in wisteria and ivy; and the large houses are unkempt or abandoned. We stagger through the village to find a shop as we are self-catering tonight and need to find supplies for supper and breakfast. There is a small organic bio-store, where we purchase muesli and yoghurt, both by weight (breakfast), and bananas and cheese and pâté and fresh bread (supper) and red wine. We stuff it all into our backpacks and retrace our steps to the restaurant by the church, intending to have a delicious French *plat du jour*. It's more of a workman's caff; but handwritten sign promises *galettes* and a *formule* of three courses for €15.

There are several tables under the awning by the road; one by the door into the bar has four workmen enjoying copious quantities of wine with their meal, the single table next to them has someone who looks like a travelling salesman. We sit down at an empty table in front of them, but the waitress comes rushing out and tells us it's reserved. The others are not set, but she quickly flings red paper mats, cutlery and glasses on to a little table at the front by the road.

'*Formule?*' she asks.

I shake my head. '*Non; galette, s'il vous plaît.*'

But she shakes her head. 'It's not possible today. There's *formule menu du jour*, just today's set menu.'

I point to the sign promising *galettes*.

But she still shakes her head. '*Non*, just *formule.*'

'No menu?'

'No, no menu.'

So we order two *formules*, with a beer for Kim. She brings bread, water, the charcuterie starter.

'I didn't know Spam is still made,' Kim remarks wryly. A large white plate holds a small lump of rough terrine, a couple of slices of bright pink processed meat, tiny snippets of pistachios, a cornichon.

Another man arrives and a small front table hastily laid for him. Our waitress returns with three main courses, balanced on her arms, for him and ourselves; the greasy juices are running everywhere, down her arm, on to the floor and on to the table when she places the plates down. Each plate has a single large leg of chicken, herbed and roasted, and a pile of *frites*, all floating.

'*Bon appetite!*' she wishes us cheerfully.

'Vegetables?' I plead. 'Or salad?'

She brings a bowl of a few limp lettuce leaves and three slices of tomato, drizzled with a dark shiny brown dressing. Meanwhile, the group arrive for the reserved table – a large voluble man, two medium-sized men who grunt in unison at his long, loud stories, and one thin small young man who keeps very quiet. I watch as they are served steak, and a lovely looking luscious salad and *frites*, *brebis* cheese with fig jam, *iles flottante*.

We are not allowed cheese, we are told, as it's not on the *formule*. And our *iles flottante* are disgusting: a very thin yellow custard topped with two mounds of tough bitter whipped egg whites with a soupçon of caramel drizzled across. Kim manfully eats his while I go on to Trip Advisor and write a very realistic review.

'Coffee?' we say, hopefully.

But no, the coffee machine broke earlier this morning.

So much for wonderful French cuisine.

We give up and leave, and find what is now the perfect riverside path; the river flowing swiftly on our left, pretty houses and cottages on our right. But Kim is struggling.

'Maybe the *iles flottante* weren't a good idea,' I suggest helpfully. He says it's his legs and he finds ibruprofen to take while I relieve him of tonight's wine and cheese and put them into my rucksack to try to ease his load a little. Eventually the path culminates at a large modern bridge; underneath it is a boat and bike hire – a large wooden shack, with a little café, outside picnic benches, and coffee and ice cream. We sit and indulge.

Kim soon feels much better, revived by sugar and caffeine, and we are able to head away from the river to Josse, a small hamlet with a BnB for the night. Plane trees line the road, their trunks beautifully stippled and coloured. Turning into the driveway of a modern house set back across expansive lawns with children's swings and slides, piles of wood stacked neatly by the back door, we wonder what the room will be like. It turns out to be the distant garage – converted last year, apparently, into two rooms, and the main door replaced with big bi-fold glass doors. The first room is the living room, with white modern furniture, a full kitchen down the right-hand wall, including a dishwasher, a big white sofa on the left wall, and a round table and chairs in the middle. A gap leads into the bedroom, filled with an enormous double bed covered with bright Indian fabric and with glittery mirrors and reflective lights on the walls. Another door from that leads into the shower room which boasts a washing machine. I am so excited to see it, something I take for granted at home. The clothes are soon all in the machine; we don't need to go out again as we have supper with us. I shower; Kim sleeps.

I hope he can make it tomorrow.

KIM:

That was one of the hardest days for me. Several times I wondered if I would be able to keep going. I'm not quite sure what the reason was, but hopefully the adrenaline will kick in tomorrow to get us over the finishing line at Cap Breton. I'm buoyed up, of course, by the news that Germany are out of the World Cup. And England is still in. What's more, it was South Korea in whom we have a distinct interest (our son-in-law is originally from Seoul) who did the damage. Well done SK!

And so we spend a night in a converted garage.

Chapter Twelve
Finding Ourselves in France

The Last Day

June 28th is Day 27 of walking across France. Kim is up early. I vaguely hear him in the bathroom, in the kitchen, brewing coffee, filling flasks. I've slept for nine hours yet I am slow to regain full consciousness. Lots of coffee does eventually return me to the land of the living and our 'bio' breakfast of muesli, *brebis* yoghurt (sheep's milk) and fresh apricots is wonderfully fortifying. We are tramping along the road by 8am – Kim had been up early, raring to go! He is fortunately on fine form again; the blister on my sixth toe is agony.

I can hardly believe this really is the last day. There is excitement and anticipation, tinged with regret and sadness that it will all too soon be at an end. Kim navigates carefully along back roads, through the outskirts of villages, trying to avoid cars as much as possible. The second village has a modern tiny strip mall of shops, one of which is billed as an artisanal *pâtisserie* and it has a few small tables and chairs outside. Time for an early elevenses? There's more of those delicious *croissants aux amandes*, and we are allowed to drink our own coffee, as they don't have a coffee machine. So we sit outside – and the rain begins.

'Might as well finish in the way it's been most of the time,' Kim says.

By mid-morning we are halfway, still passing field after field of maize. Kim cheerfully begins to sing.

'A-maize-ing grace, how sweet the sound,' as we think of amazing crops being deci-maized by rain. It seems appropriate that there should be rain on our last day, to help us remember all the rain and *boue*, mud, of the past weeks.

The sight of a gorgeous male peacock in the field beside us makes me come to a halt. He struts proudly beside the tall maize, his colourful tail bumping over the stones. It is totally random to see him here; maybe he has escaped from a stately home or a wild life park? A little further along the road and a small white van approaches us and pulls over to stop beside us. The driver, an older man with the usual nasal twang, leans out of his window, shaking his fist at us.

'You are walking on the incorrect side of the road,' he says. 'You are not facing the oncoming traffic. Move over to the other side at once.'

It's too complicated to explain why we are on that side of the road so we meekly cross over to the 'correct' side – until he is out of sight and we can cross back and continue to walk with the traffic coming from behind us.

The Sandy Forest

A quick supermarket stop to buy green mint tea and a half bottle of inexpensive celebratory Limoux bubbles for later, and then we reach the Forêt Communale de Seignosse and we are walking under exceptionally tall dark pine trees, on deep sandy tracks. It reminds us of the approach to Lady Anne's beach in north Norfolk. There are tracks going in every direction and the one we choose grows progressively more sandy; we are sinking into pale fine sand with each step and it's hard going. There are mosquitoes and more mosquitoes, and their buzz disturbs the thick pure quietness of the forest; the heady scent of the trees fills our nostrils and the sand itches at our legs.

The track peters out at a dark wooden garden gate bearing a sign: *'Privée'*.

Forlorn, we turn around, retrace out steps and try a different route, this time trying to follow paths marked on Google maps. The path goes round a bend to the left, still under the trees, still on sinking sands, and joins a slightly less sandy, wider farm track. This is easier walking, but it still feels as though we are lost somewhere in the pine woods. Another few kilometres, and suddenly we emerge at the other side of the forest. It is the main road, and immediately opposite us is a large sign.

CAP BRETON.

But Where is the Sea?

It's an amazing feeling – but there's still at least 5 kilometres to walk in order to reach the sea. After negotiating two busy roundabouts we are on to a cycle and pedestrian pathway, the road on our left, houses and fences and driveways on our right. The excitement is growing. We talk about how awful Kim had felt yesterday; how we have each had a couple of bad days – fortunately at different times. How we have been able to help one another through the bad patches. We reminisce a little but really we want to get there now.

But where is the sea? Down one little road of seaside-esque houses, along another. Suburban architecture isn't life-giving exactly but it has to be navigated, and we are grateful for the GPS. There's a marina; the clouds are low, dark grey and menacing and we still can't see the sea. Boats bob up and down; families cycle along the pathway; the horizon is edged dark with pine trees. More little streets and we try to hasten our steps, holding hands as eventually we approach the promenade, in front of us at last. It's a high concrete wall with a balustrade on the top; the sea must surely be on the other side? Walking the final few hundred yards towards the wall between tall grey buildings we want to shout to everyone that we have just arrived from the Mediterranean, that we have walked every step of over five hundred kilometres.

We race up the concrete steps on to the promenade, back packs banging against our backs; and there it is.

The Atlantic

We have made it.

The grey, heaving Atlantic Ocean lies below us, across a deeply sloping shingle beach. Going down the steps on to the yellow gritty sandy gravel, we look for someone to take a photo of us but the place is deserted.

'Let's stop and give thanks to God,' I suggest, and we thank him for safety on the walk, for healing and restoration, for bringing us here and drawing us closer together on the way. My heart is surging with relief, with excitement, with the completion of the adventure.

Scrambling down towards the ocean, up over a ridge of shingle and then below us is a grey-and-pink tartan rug, with two young women sitting chatting. Kim approaches them and explains what we have just done and their excitement levels join ours. The dark-haired one leaps up and offers to take our photo. And suddenly the excitement bursts out!

Kim and I laugh and cry and laugh some more; he opens the Limoux and I shriek with joy as he holds it to my lips.

WE HAVE DONE THIS! We have made it. We really have walked from the Mediterranean to the Atlantic. And here we are.

I think I do a little dance.

Kim carries the bottle to the water's edge and stands in the shallows – and realises his boots have holes in the bottom too. But it no longer matters. We are stunned with the achievement; we laugh and cry and kiss and hold hands, and the camera whirls as the young French girl follows us recording our joy and thrill.

We have just walked right across France.

We really have walked here from the Mediterranean.

Sauntering back along the beach, the dull grey ocean on our left, we head towards Nina's Restaurant and lunch. The sun tries to beam on us as we claim a table outside at the front of the restaurant overlooking the promenade and the beach. Kim orders two glasses of real Champagne and we raise our glasses to toast each other, with more tears and smiles and emotion. It's a long, leisurely lunch; we have nowhere else we'd rather be, no further destination we have to reach. We watch people walking along the old jetty, opened by Napoleon in 1858; we look at each other and smile. And look and smile again with tears in our eyes.

A couple of hours later, we hobble along the seafront, gazing at the shops selling beach balls and sun loungers and suntan lotion. Cap Breton reminds us of small seaside towns of our childhood, low seafront houses built in the sixties, ice creams and surfboards, families and children and dogs. At the end is our hotel. We stiffly mount the steps and go in through the glass doors. We want to tell everyone what we have just done! Instead, we tell the two receptionists and as we do, my tears begin again and one of them produces a box of tissues for me. They probably think we are mad old people. We book massages for tomorrow and retire to our room, intending to take a siesta.

But we are too pumped! The adrenaline is still flowing and the information on the town's brochure says it has a range of shops including shoes and clothes. So we unpack, shower, make a cup of tea – and then decide to head for the shops and meander in the town and treat ourselves to a celebratory new outfit each – we are both totally fed up with the two non-walking outfits we've alternated each evening.

We can still scarcely believe what we have done. We have walked across France. And I have the most enormous and painful blister on the end of my left foot to prove it.

KIM:
What an emotional experience! I didn't realise how much we had invested in this until we got here. A much easier walk today and a spring in our steps. I'm so proud of my lovely wife. She's a stayer and a keeper in oh so many ways.

Kim and I each post the achievement on social media; our son sends us the clip of Forest Gump: *'I think I might go home now . . .'* There are literally hundreds of congratulatory messages – I don't think either of us had realised how many people were following our adventures when we posted each day.

'Yeah, yeah, all of that is good,' writes an American friend, 'but what I want to know is what are we all supposed to do with the rest of our summer now we can't follow your adventure anymore? I say you should turn around and walk back . . . '

'Thanks for sharing the journey with us – thanks for your honesty and inspiration – how beautiful on the mountain are the feet of him who bring good news, who proclaim peace, who bring good tidings, who proclaim salvation, who say to Zion, your God reigns!'

'What a feat . . . !'

I post a photo of my feet. 'But your nail varnish is unchipped! I am in awe!'

And a photo of the 'luxury' items I deemed necessary to bring: a string of pearls, nail varnish, lipstick, mascara.

Then I sleep for ten hours.

How Was It for You?

For twenty-four days plus three rest days, we have walked. Walked across France. The calm and the sun of the Canal du Midi. The undulations of the Ariège and then the beautiful Gers with few centres of civilisation but with a lot of mud. *Boue.* Mud, rain and mud. There was rain down our necks, mud on our boots, thick slimy mosquito-infested pluff mud. Everywhere. The fields were inundated, the maize dying, the ditches full, the edges slipping away. And occasionally, glimpses of the snow-capped Pyrenees, accompanying us on our left. And more maize. Not once did we arrive on market day anywhere – so much for thinking we would enjoy delicious picnics of fresh cheese and fruit from the local market stalls.

And the people. Warm, friendly, hospitable. We learned so much from them. Of the relief to be welcomed in and blessed even though we were total strangers, walk-weary and dishevelled. That the smallest things can make an enormous difference when given with care and solicitude. That the things that usually matter so much to me are not the most important after all. That I can squat on a grass verge anywhere if necessity dictates – if I turn my head so I can't see anyone passing, they can't see me either, right? That I can walk even when it's painful.

You can do anything if you need to or have to.

And the most important thing for us to learn, perhaps: that two are better than one, for if one falls, each can help the other up (Ecclesiastes 4:10).

All those days, all that distance. All the laughs and the tears, the uncomfortable beds and the strange places we found ourselves, the spectacular countryside, the fascinating conversations. And one happy, tired, jubilant couple.

Who have, as hoped, found themselves in France.

Post-Perambulation

We have been home again for two weeks. It feels strange in some ways. Two weeks of trying to settle back in, catch up with family and friends, find a new normal. I miss the simplicity of each day having one main focus: walking to the next accommodation, with nothing else to worry about. The simplicity of not having to think about everyday routines such as shopping, cooking, what to wear, jobs to do. Most of all, I miss the constant companionship of spending each day with my husband, with a common goal, uniting in what we do and how we do it. And it's hot. Daily temperatures in the upper twenties, constant sunshine and long summer days. It is the most unusual weather this summer – wet in France and hot in England. Even the nights here are hotter than midday was in France.

It's Friday. We have promised ourselves that Friday is our walking date. Today, our forty-first wedding anniversary, we drive south for a few miles and take a circular route with Mells as the halfway point. I have another new pair of walking boots – half a size larger – and as I ease my feet into them and tie the long laces, the familiarity is good and the excitement returns. This is what we do. We walk together.

It's a pretty hike across the Somerset countryside, although the earth is cracked and the fields are dry and brown. Deep fissures open up across the tracks; there's a hosepipe ban in some parts of the country. We are still amazed at how different the arid countryside looks after the lushness of the green wet fields of south-west France.

We talk and reflect and remember; we remind one another of what it was like – favourite moments, scary moments, helpful people who blessed us. We reaffirm the new decision to have a weekly walk, to do things together, to step out into the rest of our lives as a team. It feels good to have this total day off once a week, to find ourselves again.

I think it was Anne Morrow Lindbergh who wrote something about one perfect day giving clues for a more perfect life.

We have lunch in the sunshine sitting in the courtyard of The Talbot Inn at Mells and there is that sense of wanting to tell everyone what we have recently accomplished. I'm still exultant with the sense of achievement: we walked across France! There is laughter as we recall the happy memories, fun as we walk together and follow the footpaths marked on the English map, affection as we pause at the kissing gates and exchange a kiss each time. All too soon we are back at the car but the sense of elation from a Friday walk of some fourteen miles stays with us over the next few days. We are happy and affectionate with one another. I am enjoying feeling fit and toned, ready for what lies ahead.

The adventure of the Grand Walk has proved to be the most healing thing we could have done and we are blessed to have had the time and the energy that was needed for it.

Thanks overflows and thrills our hearts.

It's so enjoyable to come before you with uncontainable praises spilling from our hearts! . . . At each and every sunrise we will be thanking you for your kindness and your love. As the sun sets and all through the night, we will keep proclaiming, "You are so faithful!" . . . No wonder I'm so glad; I can't keep it in! Lord, I'm shouting with glee over all you've done, for all you've done for me!' (Psalm 92:1–4 The Passion Translation)

I hope you've enjoyed walking across France with us! You might also enjoy reading and seeing more about my walks and pilgrimages, or receiving my emails with ideas on how to deepen your walk with God – however long, short or non-existent your physical walking! You can find all this on my blog at ministriesbydesign.org where I write about finding God, about walking, about books I've enjoyed, or about anything else that I find helpful! And you can follow me on Facebook (Penelope Swithinbank) or Instagram (penelopeswithinbank) or Twitter (@ minstriesbydsgn)

Useful Lists, Stats and Numbers

Numbers

342/547 miles/kilometres walked

24 days of walking

3 rest days

24 daily walks planned

25 accommodations

4 times someone wanted to go home

0 fresh markets seen – we never arrived anywhere on market day

2 pairs of boots worn through

£3000 raised to divide between International Justice Mission and People against Poverty

2 tired jubilant people

1 pair of new boots a size too small

1 foot operation in November – but it was so worth it!

And one of the hottest summers on record back at home in England

Things I was glad to have with me

Tiny umbrella

Eau de cologne cooling stick

Small special absorbent towel (mopping brow, drying hands/feet)

Camping washing line with inbuilt 'peg' system

Walking pole

Foot creams – energising/healing
Mosquito/fly spray for rooms and for outdoors
Toecaps
Journal and pen
Kindle, loaded with books, liturgies, Bible
Tumble-dryer sheets to layer in-between clothes for a fresher scent
French chargers for electronics
Lipstick, nail varnish and mascara
Waterproof inner bags for packing things separately
Easy-dry clothes – outer and under
Sunhat/rain hat

Highlights

Funniest moment
P – *pas de menu* in Eugènie-le-Bains.
K – *les evacuations* (P's squatting sessions!)

Worst moment
P – the daily final kill-o-metre
K – totally stuck climbing over the fallen tree

Scariest moment
P – the Alsatian dog attacking us
K – lost in the woods above Carcassonne

Toughest moment
P – the last hours into Eugènie-le-Bains
K – shin pains in the first few days

Most emotional moment
P & K – lunch by the Atlantic

Mileage

Day		
	1	13.88 miles
	2	12.83
	3	13.80
	4	18.14
	5	13.8 plus evening = 16.54
	6	rest day: 4.70
	7	14.5 plus evening = 15.96
	8	15.20
	9	10.67
	10	10.00
	11	11.40 plus evening =12.79
	12	13.95
	13	rest day: 1.00
	14	13.13
	15	16.31 halfway
	16	14.17
	17	14.00
	18	15.22
	19	12.21 100 miles to go!
	20	rest day
	21	18.70
	22	19.50
	23	12.30
	24	16.60
	25	14.60 plus evening = 17.21
	26	14.25
	27	16.00 plus shopping = 19.50
	28	and breathe . . .